CW01674278

Welsh Quilting Design

with Sandie Lush

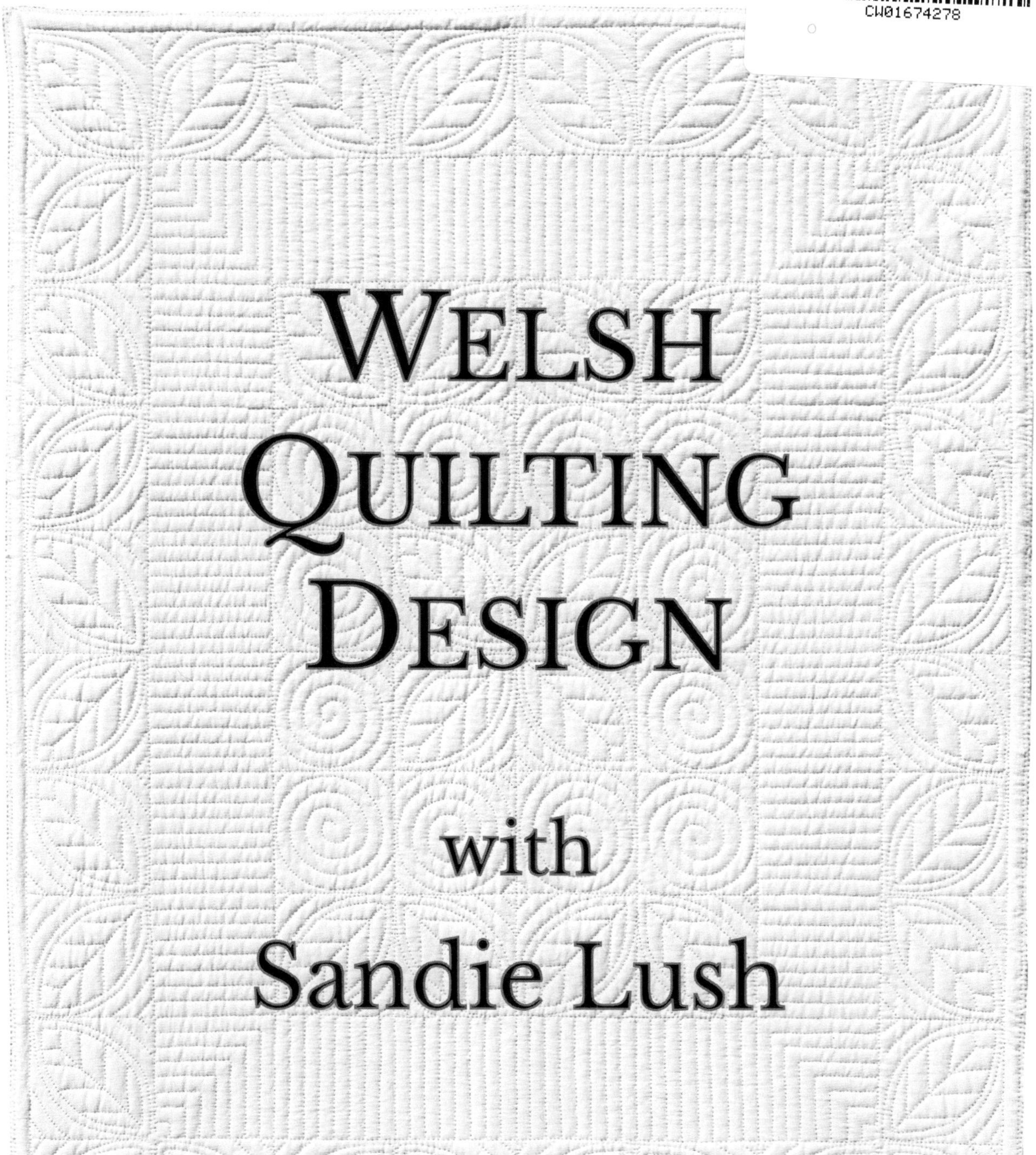

Dawns Flodau (reverse) *Sandie Lush 2016*

Copyright © 2018 by Sandie Lush; www.sandielush.co.uk; www.wholeclothquilts.biz

Sandie Lush has asserted her right to be identified as author of this work in accordance with the Copyright, Design and Patents Act of 1988. All rights reserved. No part of this publication may be reproduced, stored in a retrieval system, or transmitted, in any form or by any means, electronic or mechanical, by photocopying, recording or otherwise, without prior permission in writing.

All images copyright David Lush unless otherwise stated.

Published by Sandie Lush Designs; printed by CreateSpace.

ISBN: 978-1-9164495-0-3

Suo Gân *Sandie Lush 2009*

Contents

Tarian Aur *Sandie Lush 1999*

Foreword

While in most parts of Great Britain quilting traditions have evolved over time, Welsh quilters have been happy to stay true to the centuries old format of a central medallion surrounded by a series of borders.

In Wales many quilts were made by itinerant quilters who worked from farm to farm. Their knowledge was not necessarily passed on when they stopped working and consequently many patterns and skills were lost. However, in isolated valleys quilt-wives carefully maintained the tradition, but their isolation (and often ensuing poverty) meant this wonderful design style has, on several occasions, nearly died out. Each time a revival has been sparked by passionate individuals with a determination to see the craft continue.

The most inspirational champion of Welsh quilts in recent times has been American Jen Jones who, over the past 45 years, has acquired an impressive collection of Welsh quilts and blankets. In 2008, she and her husband Roger Clive-Powell transformed Lampeter Town Hall into The Welsh Quilt Centre. From the following year until the end of 2018 Jen shared some of her vast collection in a series of stunning exhibitions, attracting visitors from all over the world.

Jen's quilts have been an inspiration to many, including the author of this book, motivating them to design and make their own Welsh quilts. It is also through Jen's encouragement that this book has been written in the hope it will provide insight and inspiration for others to continue in this wonderful and unique quilting tradition.

Sandie Lush 2018

Tarian Aur detail *Sandie Lush 1999*

Dadeni *Sandie Lush 2017*

Introduction

Welsh quilts are prized for their distinctive quilting patterns and wool filling, both of which combine to give the finished quilts a sculptural quality.

Most Welsh quilts have quilting patterns set out in the traditional British style of a central medallion with a series of surrounding borders. What sets Welsh quilts apart is that these designs frequently bear no relation to the patchwork patterns or types of fabric on which they have been stitched. This, and the fact there are no set design 'rules' compared to other British quilt styles, gives Welsh quilts a reputation for being 'quirky'.

The motifs used to design these wonderful quilts were derived from a variety of sources. Motifs were often simple shapes such as a heart or leaf, both of which could easily be created by folding and cutting newspaper. Paper-folding could also be used when drawing rather than cutting out shapes and is still a popular method for creating basic templates.

Drawing around existing shapes was another simple method employed to create designs. Household items such as cotton reels, plates or a flat iron, and shapes from nature such as leaves, were all used in this way. As well as from the natural world, other designs came from the traditional patterns carved into oak panels and furniture, or from plasterwork, fabrics and even wallpaper. Unlike North country quilts, it is very unusual to see feather designs in Welsh quilts.

A favourite design resource today is patterns and motifs taken from old quilts. This is nothing new! In past times a quilter may have taken inspiration from existing quilts or even from the work of a rival quilt-wife in the next valley. A combination of motifs from several sources can give an entirely new look to old designs.

When working in an old-fashioned quilt frame, it was possible to draw around templates and household items directly onto the fabric using chalk. A design could be pre-planned, but often evolved as the quilt progressed. Less experienced quilters often found this led to asymmetry of design and the necessary addition of an extra part-motif to fill an unexpected space. It also frequently led to asymmetry of shape - there are very few truly square Welsh quilts. Again, this lack of symmetry added to the reputation of Welsh quilts being 'quirky'.

Some quilts were designed on paper before the pattern was transferred onto fabric. It is this approach which is more common today as, not only is it more accurate, it is easier to alter a paper design than try to remove or modify lines marked on the quilt top itself.

This book aims to help the reader create their own original designs, from the creation of simple motifs through to using them in increasingly complex ways to create larger Welsh motifs and traditional Welsh quilting patterns.

The motifs used to illustrate this process have been adapted from designs garnered from a variety of sources over many years. A selection of these motifs can be found in the Appendix.

Getting Started

Creating designs on paper rather than directly onto fabric permits changes to be made easily, allowing a design to gradually evolve into the finished product.

At the design stage only a quarter of the finished pattern needs to be created, but when subsequently tracing the design onto the fabric, it is easier to work with a half-master rather than a quarter-master pattern. Initially, a sheet of tracing or thin drawing paper large enough to accommodate one quarter of the required finished size of the quilt is required. The second quarter can then be copied from this at a later stage.

It is possible to purchase large A1 sheets of tracing paper from art shops. A single sheet is usually large enough for a cot-sized design half-master, and joining several of these sheets together will provide an area for drawing larger quilt designs. Smaller A3 pads of tracing paper can be bought from stationers, but will then require more pieces to be joined together.

A more practical (and economical) way to create a larger piece of tracing paper is by using a roll of greaseproof paper from the local supermarket. It is better to find a brand that has not been treated with silicone, as this treatment provides a non-stick surface that may be extremely useful when baking, but is equally unhelpful when trying to join pieces together with Sellotape.

When joining together greaseproof or tracing paper pieces, butt the machine-cut edges together rather than edges that have been cut at home. This ensures a tight fit which should be joined at intervals a few inches apart with Sellotape. Magic Tape is particularly useful for this at it can be repositioned easily and has a matt surface which can be drawn on.

Once the machine-cut edges are secure, the gaps between pieces of tape can be filled in with more tape. This approach will not distort the paper, whereas attempting to join the edges with a continuous piece of tape usually does.

Very little other equipment is needed. A pencil and eraser are required for drawing during the design stage, and extra tracing paper may be needed to create templates and to experiment with ideas. Paper scissors are also useful if cutting out motif shapes.

A quilting ruler is ideal for creating the equidistant parallel lines often used in filling patterns. A normal ruler can be used for this, but drawing will take slightly longer as parallel distances will need to be marked out at intervals before the marks are joined together to form the line.

Curved lines and circles can be drawn around household items such as plates, cups, cotton reels etc. or by using technical drawing equipment such as compasses or a rolling ruler.

To facilitate tracing the design onto the fabric ready for quilting, the completed pattern can be inked over with a fine-line permanent black marker. If this inking process is carried out on the unused (clean) side of the tracing paper, pale coloured fabrics will not acquire unwanted pencil marks; however, asymmetric motifs such as spirals will be reversed.

The fabric can then be placed and pinned onto the finished pattern and the design traced on with a water soluble artists' pencil or crayon, or other suitable marker.

Simple Welsh Designs

Dawns Flodau *Sandie Lush 2016*

Creating Basic Motifs

Templates were often created using brown paper or newspaper. This paper-cutting method is very useful for customising shapes to exactly fit into a required space.

Folding a piece of paper in half before cutting out a shape ensures that both halves of the motif are the same.

Symmetrical drawings can be created using the same approach. A half motif can be drawn and the paper folded in half along the centre of the motif. The rest of the motif can then be traced on the reverse side of the fold.

Heart motifs (above) and leaf shaped motifs (below) can easily be created this way.

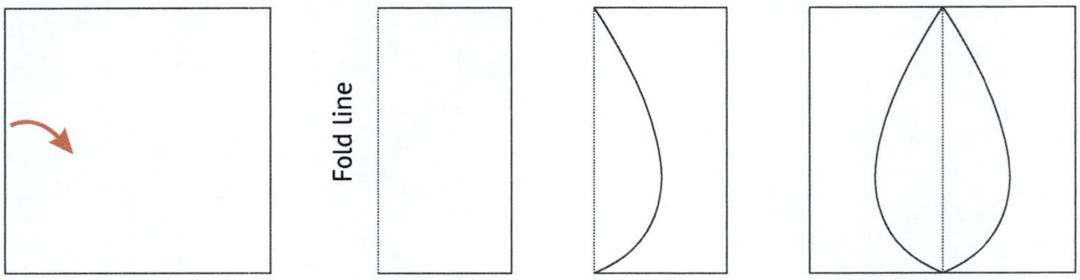

By folding the paper into four, the leaf shape created would be completely symmetrical.

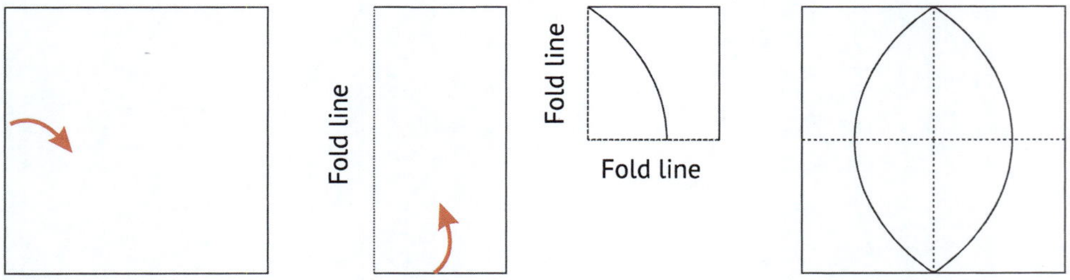

Rose and star shapes can also be made by folding and cutting paper.

Fold the paper in half and then into a quarter as before.

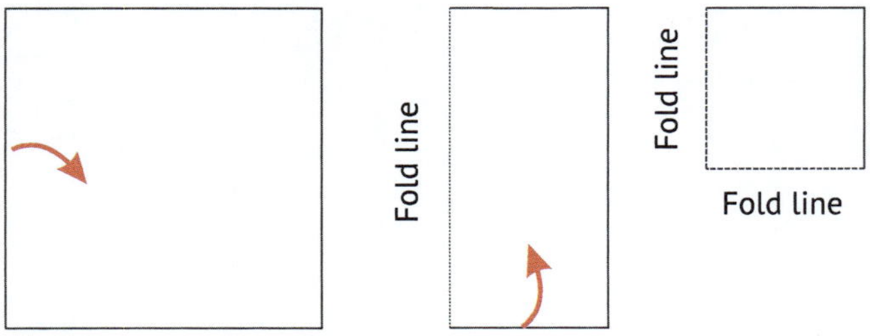

This square is then folded on the diagonal and the resultant triangle folded across so that the bottom edges lie along the diagonal fold.

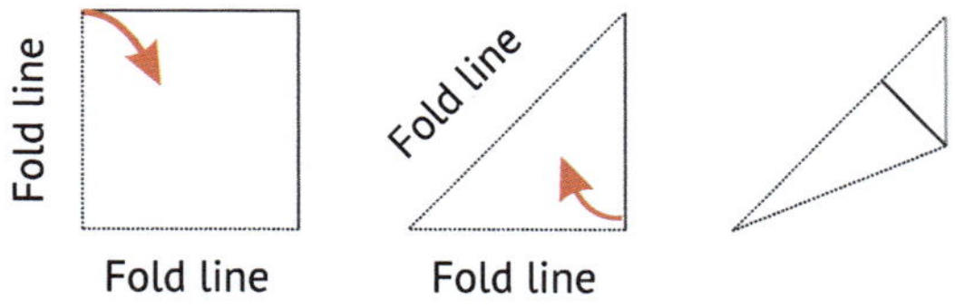

Drawing or cutting only half the petal shape ensures that each of the eight outer petal shapes is symmetrical.

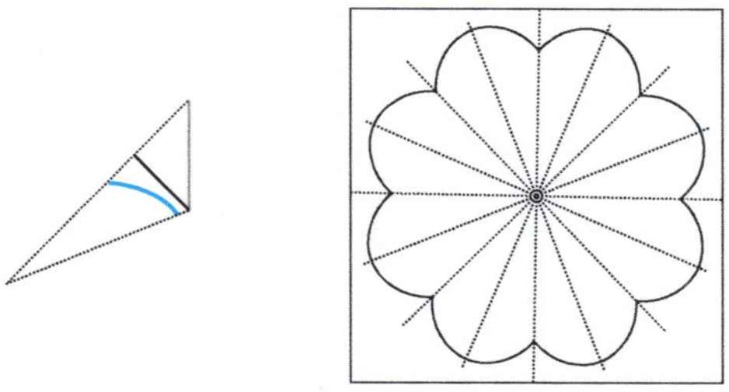

By making a straight diagonal cut rather than a curved one, star shapes can also be formed.

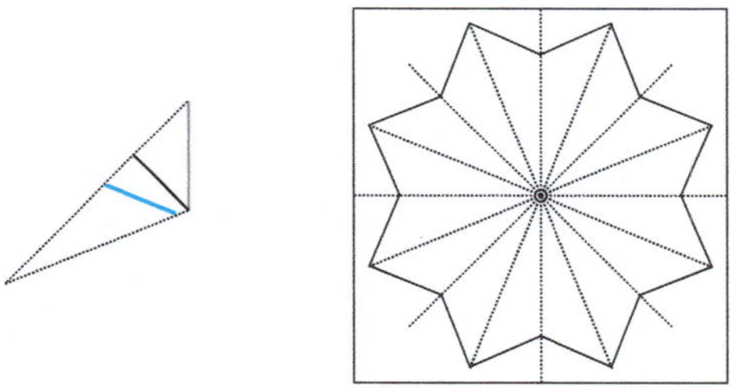

Both rose and star motifs can be positioned rotated through 22.5 degrees.

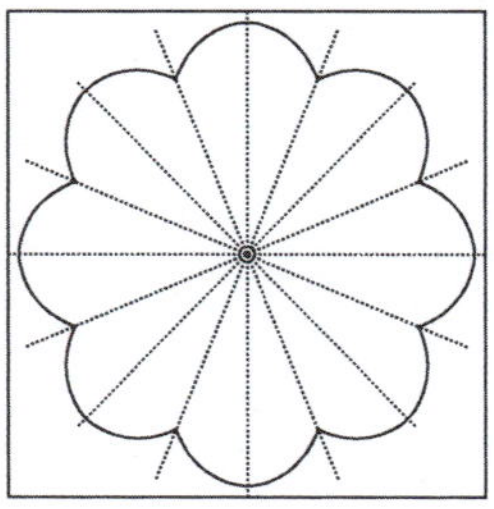

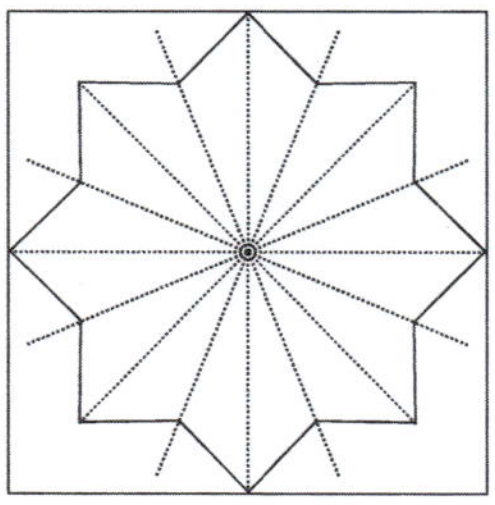

Other popular motifs such as the paisley pear and bent leaf would have been drawn freehand. Generally, motifs were (and still are) outlined with an echo line to define their shape.

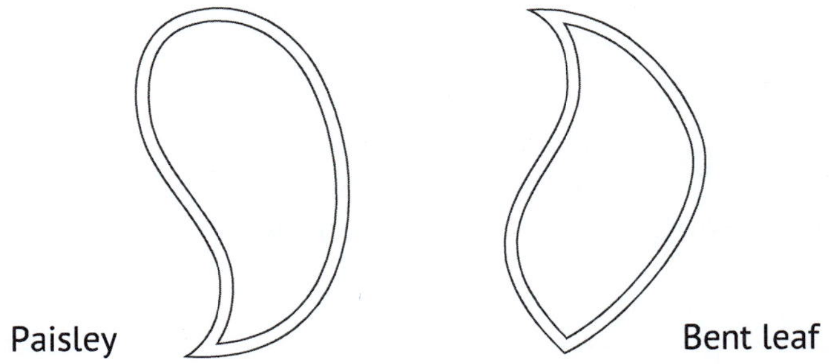

The inner spaces of a motif can be filled with a variety of smaller motifs and fillings. For example, the symmetrical leaf shape can be filled with echo lines or veins, and the heart with a simple grid.

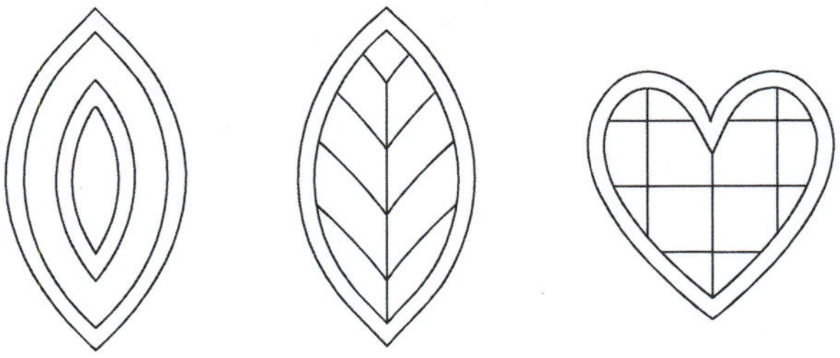

Further examples of how these motifs can be filled can be found on page 29.

Spirals are the Celtic symbol of life everlasting and feature extensively in Welsh quilts in a wide range of sizes.

Their appearance is distinct from the spirals found in quilts from the North East of England (the other regional area famous for its unique quilting designs and wholecloth quilts). Those Durham spirals open out as they increase in size whereas Welsh spirals nearly always have lines that are spaced an equal distance apart.

Welsh spirals can be drawn by joining a series of circles together at the same point of the circle with each rotation.

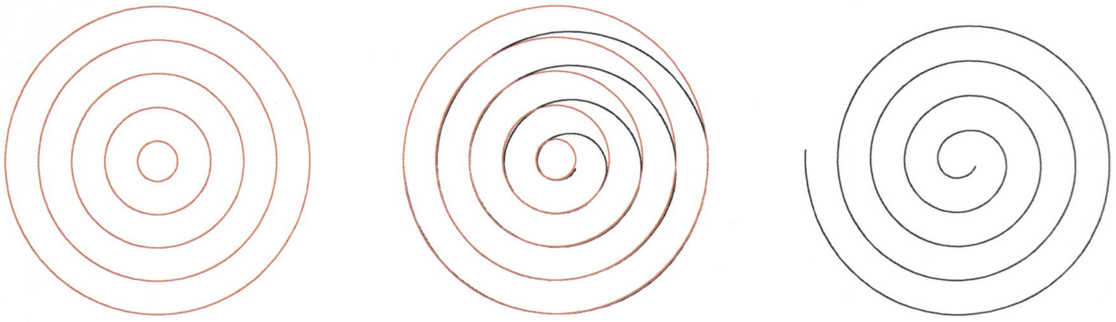

Designing Using a Grid

Dawns y Dail *Sandie Lush 1998*

Using a Grid

There are several ways in which the design of Welsh quilting patterns can be approached.

Probably the easiest method is to assemble motifs into a grid formation. This grid could be made up of squares of any size, but to allow the novice designer to start on a smaller project such as a cushion, it is suggested that a 4" square is used.

Using a 4" scale, four boxes will form the centre design of a cushion and sixteen boxes will create a whole cushion pattern.

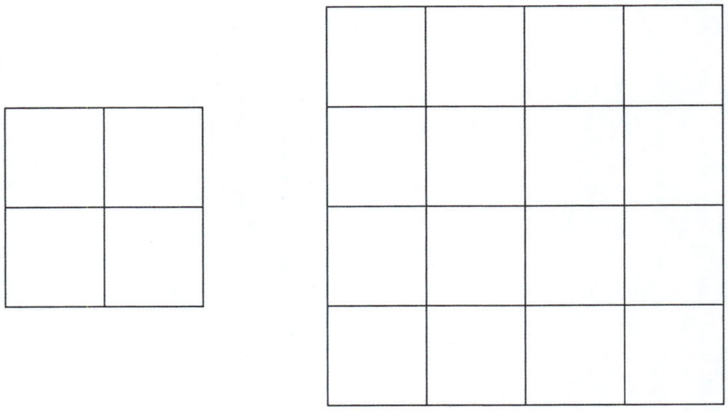

Here are three simple traditional Welsh motifs chosen to fill the grid.

The heart and leaf motifs have been sized to exactly fit a 4" box when they are placed at an angle of 45 degrees.

Filling each of the sixteen boxes with the leaf shape will give an all-over design.

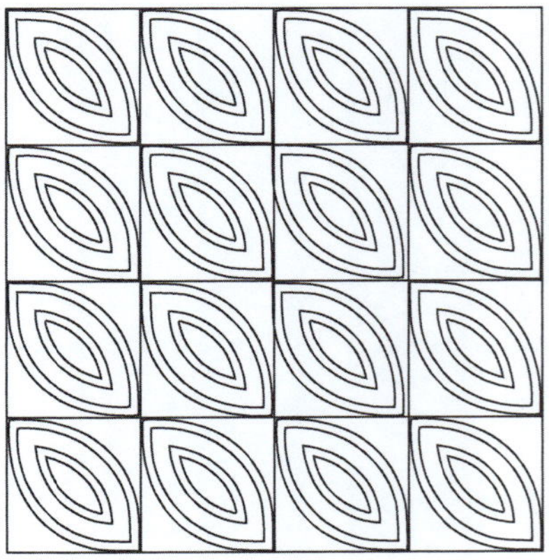

However, rotating the leaf expands the range of design possibilities.

Consider just the centre four squares.

These could contain leaves which can be rotated to form a circle.

They could also be rotated to form a cross.

A

B

Either of these patterns could then be repeated to give whole cushion designs.

Design A

Design B

If designing with all sixteen squares at once, placing the leaves in different orientations will give other variations.

Simply swapping the centres of the two examples above will result in alternative designs.

Border of design A, centre of design B

Border of design B, centre of design A

Three basic motifs were shown at the beginning of this section, but so far only one has been used. The addition of a new motif will add variety to the design.
The original four-leaf centres could be surrounded by spirals which can be rotated into subtly different border patterns.

Centre A with spiral border

Centre B with spiral border

The arrangement of spirals and leaves can also be placed in a variety of orientations, thus creating different centre and border forms...

Border of design A with centre spirals

Border of design B with centre spirals

...or indeed a wealth of other designs.

Design A with corner spirals

Design B with centre and corner spirals

This method could be taken further and used to design a whole quilt.

A 24" x 24" wall hanging could easily be created using this 4" grid method.

This design could be extended to make a 32" x 40" cot quilt.

Since the motifs can be positioned in many different ways, the possibilities are simply endless for larger designs and have the potential to be either modern or traditional in style.

Simple arrangements of motifs tend to produce modern looking designs.

In this example, two motifs have been alternated in rows.

By starting subsequent rows with the opposite motif to the previous row, the pattern becomes arranged in diagonal lines.

Single motifs can be mirror-imaged into pairs.

These pairs can then be alternated as in the example above.

This, again, leads to the pattern becoming arranged in diagonal lines.

The diagonal nature of this design is less obvious because the individual motifs do not all face in the same direction.

Two motifs can be also be used to create a more traditional design by adding a series of borders around a central design.

This method often results in square patterns. However, the addition of an extra row of spirals above and below the centre four heart motifs elongates the design into a rectangular cot quilt.

Adding a third motif adds even more variety and complexity to the design possibilities.

In larger quilts, the potential for variety becomes more obvious.

In the centre of this design, two motifs have each been arranged into groups of four and alternated in a nine-patch format.

The addition of an outer border using a third motif gives added interest and a more traditional look to the design.

Again, the design has been elongated by the addition of an extra row of hearts on two opposing sides of the outer border.

Here, the heart motif outer border of the previous quilt has been used to surround the central four spirals.

This has elongated the quilt design which was then made larger by the addition of leaf and spiral borders.

Another approach is to form an elongated centre design which can then be surrounded by a series of borders.

Further variation can be introduced with a change in size of one or more of the motifs within a design.

A

B

The quilt Dawns y Dail (shown on page 13) was created using this approach. In that design, selected squares in the original grid were further subdivided into four and filled with either spiral or small leaf motifs (A).

The leaves were filled differently as shown in version B.

These motifs were arranged in increasingly complex patterns around the centre, in a fashion similar to the 'Trip Around the World' patchwork pattern.

The addition of another line a 1/4" from the middle four boxes can provide the central pattern with greater definition.

These double lines are known as tramlines and are used extensively in Welsh quilting design to delineate where one pattern ends and the next one begins.

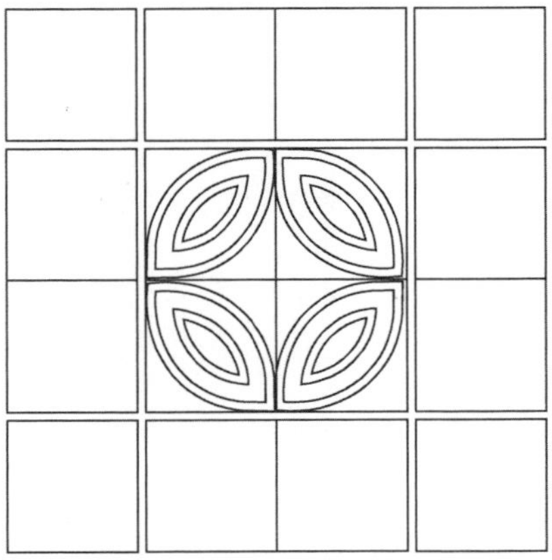

It is a matter of personal preference whether to retain all the original grid lines within a completed design. This is usually dependent on how the empty spaces between the motifs have been filled.

Filling the spaces around (and within) motifs is an important aspect of Welsh quilt design.

The grid system was used to create this silk cushion *Sandie Lush 2016*

Filling Patterns

It is important to note that quilting designs are not purely for decoration. The main function of quilting is to hold the three layers of the quilt 'sandwich' together to prevent the wadding (batting) from shifting when the quilt is washed. Therefore, quilting stitches need to be fairly evenly distributed across the quilt. The fact these lines of stitching can make beautiful patterns is an added bonus!

When designing any quilting pattern, it is important to recognise that although the quilting lines stand out on paper, the opposite applies when actually stitching the quilt, as quilting through the three layers compresses them together and makes the lines recede.

Looking at a drawing of a quilting design is rather like looking at the negative of a black and white photograph. In reality it is the gaps between the stitching lines that stand out rather than the lines themselves.

Leaving large areas unquilted not only makes it likely the quilt will become lumpy when washed, it will also shift the focus of the design. Filling these gaps with extra quilting makes a quilt more durable and, more importantly, helps give Welsh quilts their wonderful sculptured quality.

Background Fills

There is a wide range of background fillings commonly used in Welsh quilt design; from simple straight lines to more complicated grid and clamshell patterns.

Some of the most popular filling patterns are shown below:

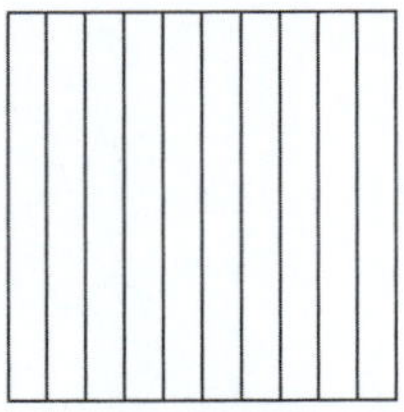
Vertical lines

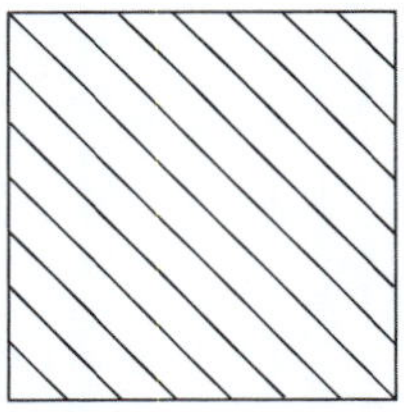
Diagonal lines

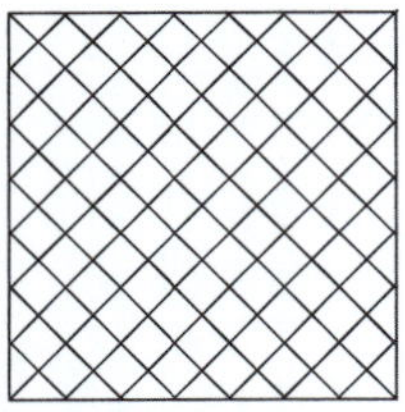
Diagonal grid

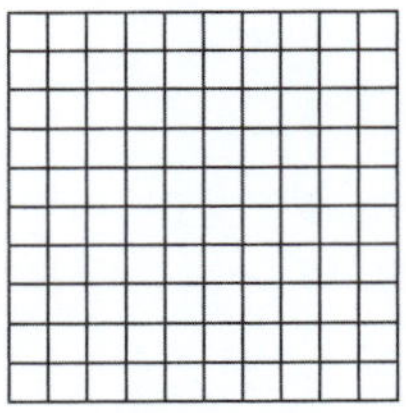
Square grid

Clamshells

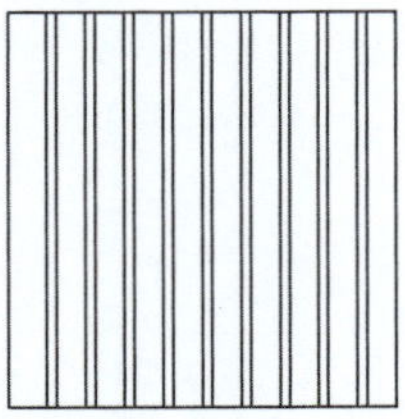
Double vertical lines

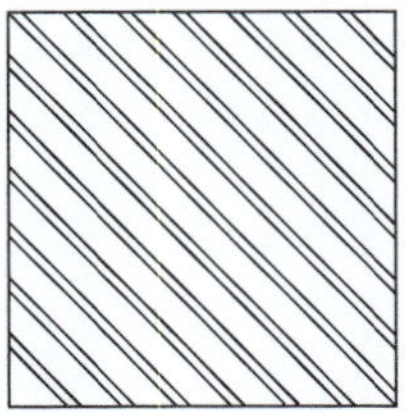
Double diagonal lines

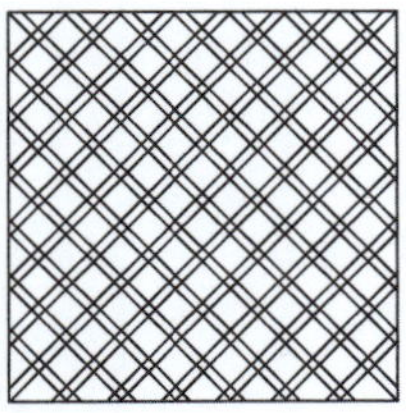
Double diagonal grid

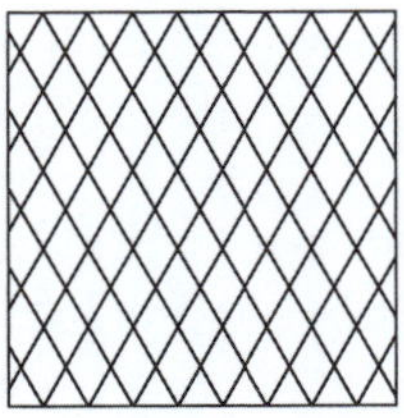
60 degree diamonds

Wineglass

Lines can vary not only in direction, but also in how far apart they are spaced. This may be anything from a 1/4" to 1 1/2" and will depend not only on the size and shape of the space to be filled but also on the size of the finished quilt.

To ensure the motif remains the focus of the design, the background pattern chosen to fill spaces around the motif should be orientated to act as a counterpoint to any filling within that motif.

Choice of background filling pattern is frequently governed by the shape that needs to be filled.

Returning to the original four-leaf patterns A and B on page 15, when the leaves are rotated to make a circle (A), the central area is left unquilted. It is important to fill this area, otherwise the empty space will stand proud and become the main focus of the design rather than the leaves surrounding it.

In this instance, the central space can be filled with either background quilting, echo lines, or another motif such as a spiral.

A

When the leaves are rotated to form a cross (B), the empty spaces are not so obvious but still need to be filled to define the outer shape of the leaf. This becomes even more important at a later stage if those leaves are surrounded by further motifs.

These fillings tend to be some form of background quilting, echo lines or small motifs.

B

When joining several smaller blocks together, the filling design can itself form a secondary pattern.

In this first example the contour lines in the spaces form diamond shapes.

In this second example, those contour lines have been adjusted around the spirals. It is preferable to only echo one of the two motifs in such a small space.

With the exception of the spiral, all the motifs in these illustrations have a second, echo line around them. This outer line is important in giving definition to the shape of the motif and helps prevent it becoming lost amongst the surrounding background quilting patterns.

Given this, it is important that any additional echo lines used as background filling are spaced differently to prevent the motif losing its outer definition.

In this example, the echo lines are spaced equally in relation to the outer edge of the leaf motif which has merged into the background design and become lost.

Here, the background echo lines are spaced at double the distance of the echo line around the motif, retaining its definition.

For example, if the echo line spacing around the motif is a 1/4", then the background echo lines would be spaced a 1/2" apart.

This is a very important aspect of Welsh quilt design and is covered in greater detail on pages 142-143.

Background filling lines can also become motifs in their own right and can be used to separate other motifs within a design.

In this design, the leaf motif has been filled with veins in place of the original echo lines.

Designs can even be created using only background patterns, although care must be taken to choose patterns that do not merge into each other.

For example, varying the angle of simple diagonal lines can give a sense of movement to a design.

A mixture of background patterns and motifs can be used to create modern, non-traditional designs.

More formal, traditional designs (which have borders arranged around a central pattern) may also be created this way.

This quilt is shown on page 9 and its reverse on page 1.

Motif Fills

Patterns used as background may also be used for filling motifs.

The original leaf shape was filled with echo lines.

However, it could also be filled with a variety of filling patterns...

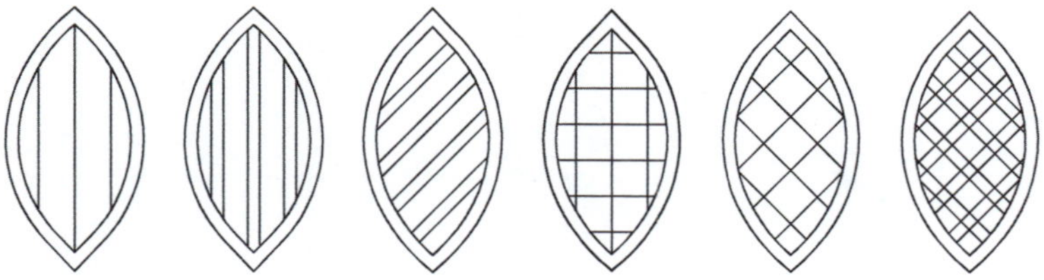

...as well as veins or other small motifs arranged to fit the space.

Depending on their placement, certain fillings (particularly asymmetric ones) can alter the appearance of the motif when it is manipulated within the grid. This provides a further opportunity to add variation.

These possibilities also hold true for the heart, paisley and bent leaf shapes.

It is this freedom of design choice that makes Welsh quilts so individual and exciting.

Another, slightly more complex way to create non-traditional patterns is by rotating the grid formation through 45 degrees to give an 'on point' design.

This will yield a slightly larger grid than previous examples. Each rotated square will measure 1.41 times the original (e.g. the original 4" square will now be just over 5.6" tall and wide).

This design approach leaves an outer of border of triangles to be filled.

To prevent this outer edge becoming lost within the overall design, the filling pattern chosen for this space needs to act in contrast to the adjacent filling patterns.

In the above example, rows of rotated squares contain a sequence of leaf, grid, spiral and concentric square fillings.

Each new horizontal row commences with the pattern that would have been next in the filling sequence at the end of the row above. This arrangement forms two diagonal patterns running top left to bottom right; one with alternating leaf and spiral motifs, the other with the two simple linear background patterns.

The outer triangles are filled with simple straight lines to contrast with the more intricate filling patterns used in the main design.

Finally, not all motifs comfortably fit within a square. Many leaf and paisley motifs are elongated and/or asymmetric in shape and better fit within a rectangular box.

Four such rectangles will form a square design when rotated around a small central square.

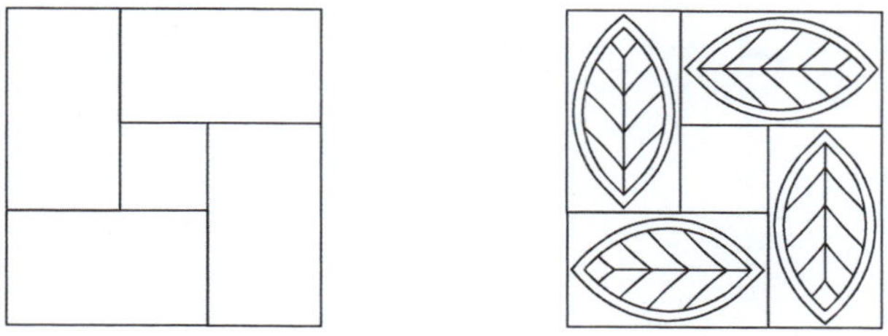

The central square can be filled with an echo or background pattern, as can the spaces around the motif within the rectangles.

The square can then be repeated to give an all-over pattern.

The design can be finished by surrounding the squares with sets of equally spaced tramlines.

Alternatively, a simple border constructed of straight lines could be added.

To ensure symmetry within each border, the lines are positioned around the centre and out to the corners. The line lengths are adjusted at the corners to form a mitred pattern. How the lines are positioned is particularly important when designing rectangular quilts as the spacing may not match at the corners.

Border Patterns

Cushion designs can be made larger by the addition of a border.

When designing quilts, it is usual to build up the overall design with border patterns. How this is achieved is explained starting on page 71.

Cables and chains

Spirals

Welsh squares

Church window

Borders can be simple chain and cable designs, or can be created by repeating motifs. Border size and complexity can vary widely. A motif can be repeated singly, doubled or can even be rotated to give a variety of border patterns.

Cables

Chain patterns can be made by laying a symmetrical leaf shape on its side.

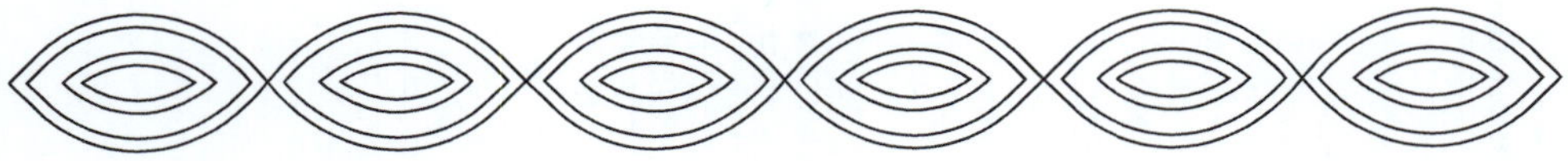

End to end

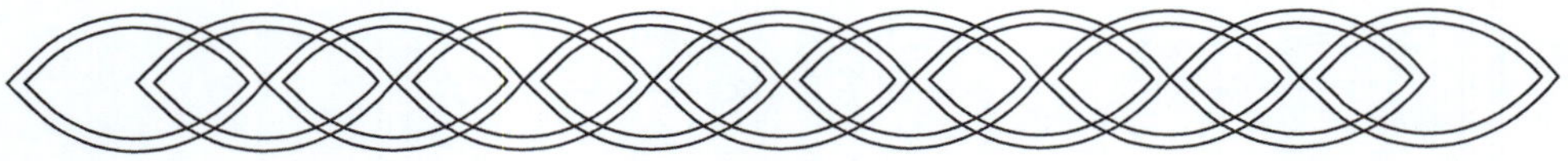

Overlapping

Partially overlapping

Overlapping the leaf shape will form continuous cable borders. How the lines defining the shapes are joined will produce different cable effects.

Cables are usually made up of two interwoven 'threads', each comprised of between three and five individual 'strands'.

The two three-stranded 'threads' illustrated here are each composed of four lines and are suitable for cot-sized designs. Five-stranded versions (composed of six lines) are more suited to bed-sized designs.

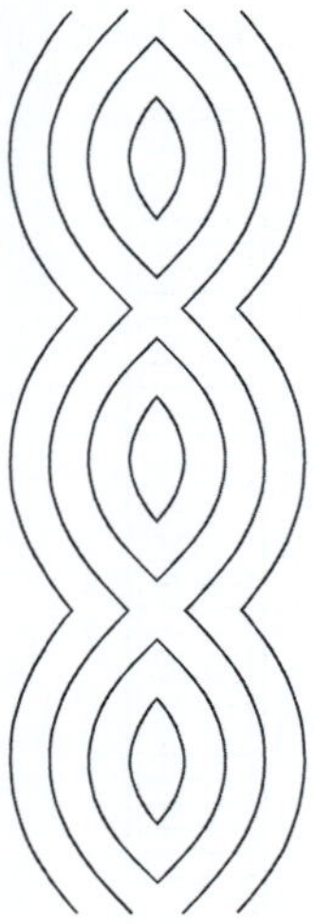

Echoed leaf shapes

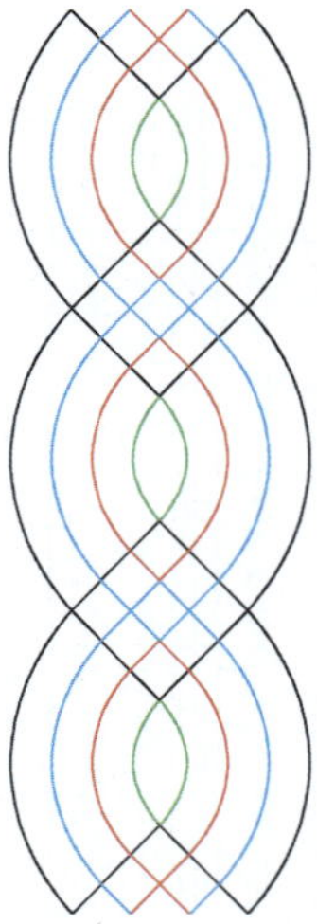

Overlapping leaves

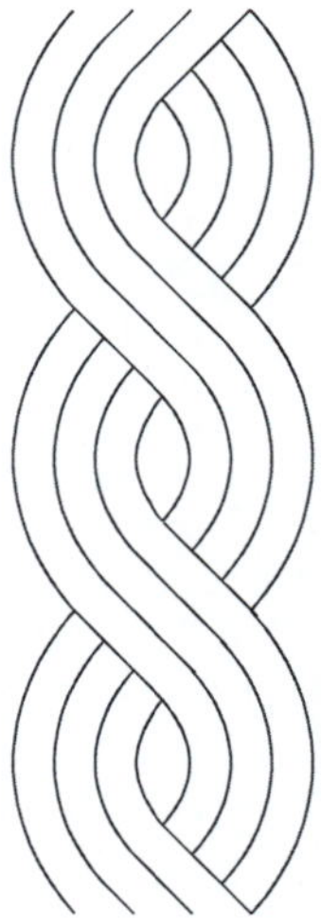

'Under/over' joins

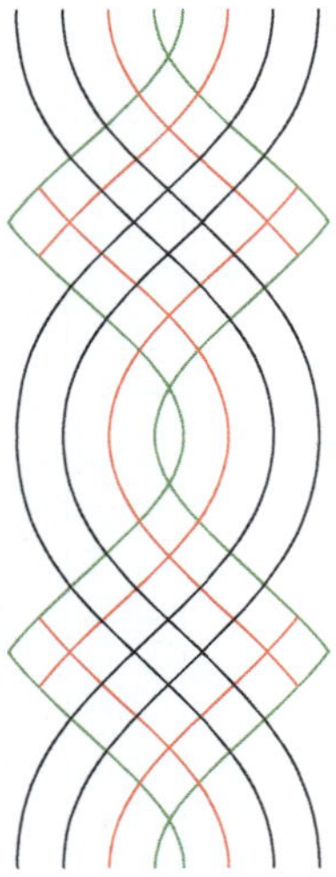

Welsh trail

The second cable was made by joining all the lines in the first cable, but can also be made by overlapping leaf shapes.

The third cable was made by removing selected lines from the second cable to form an under/over pattern.

The fourth, the Welsh trail cable, is a slightly more complex variant of cable two. How to draft this pattern is shown on page 49.

Spirals

The spiral is a favourite motif featuring in Welsh quilts and is often used to separate other design elements. Spirals can be of any size and can be spaced to fit the length of the border.

The grid system is very useful for determining the number and spacing of spirals in a border.

Spirals do not fit the border space, so...

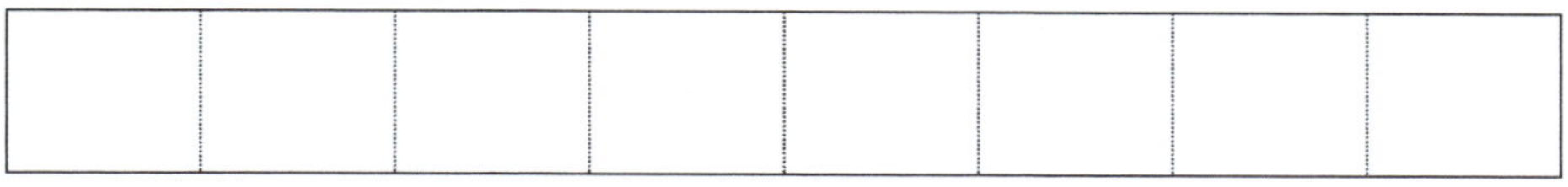

...divide the border into equal boxes...

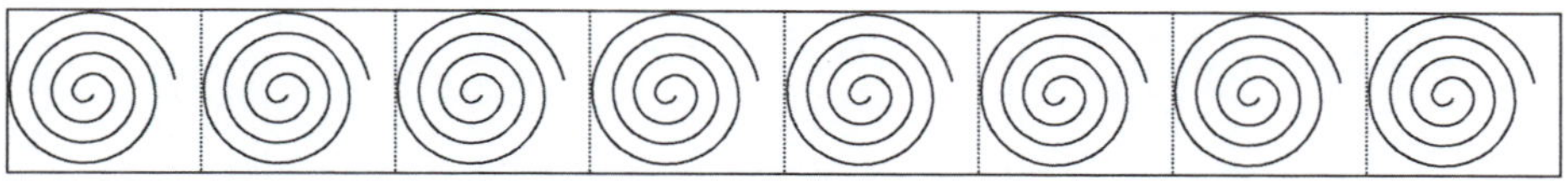

...place a spiral in each box...

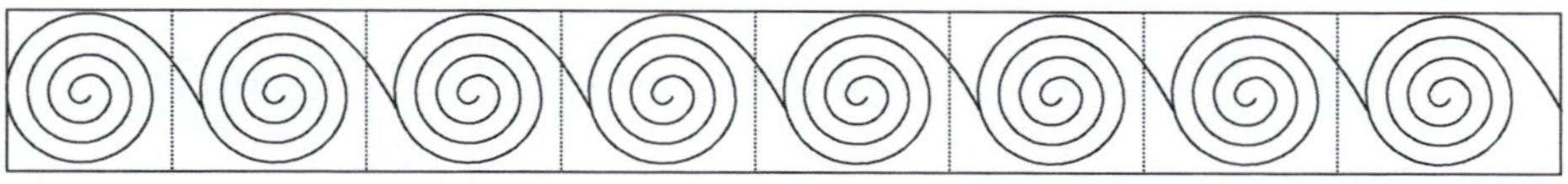

...join the spirals by extending the tails...

...remove the boxes.

Spirals may be orientated in different ways to give a range of border patterns.

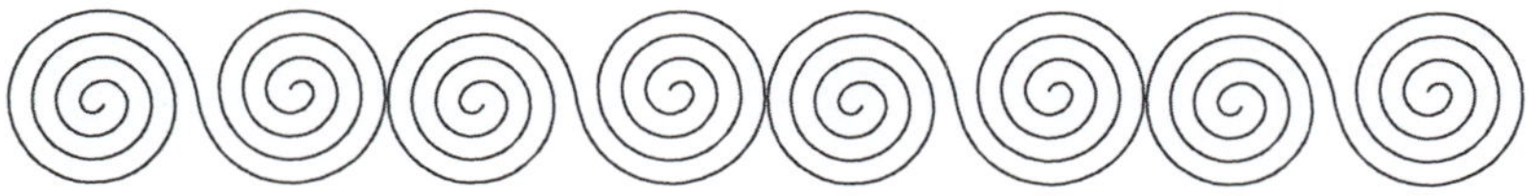

1) Over/under arrangement

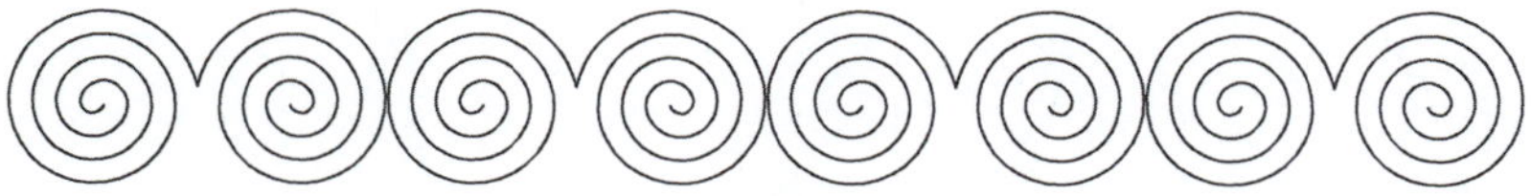

2) Mirror-imaged pairs

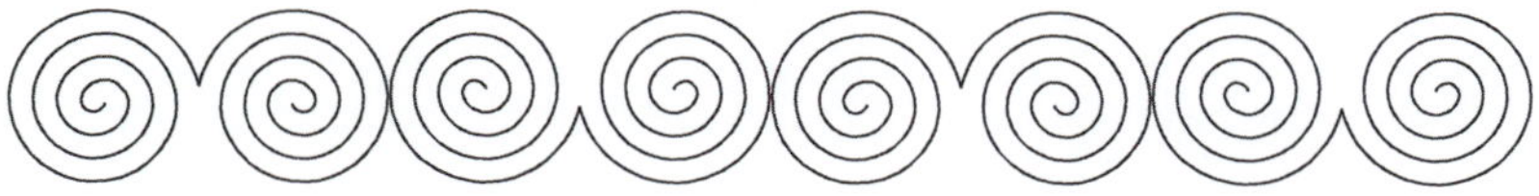

3) Over/under version of pattern 2

Larger borders can be created by ‘doubling up’ the spirals in a number of ways.

4) Mirror imaged rows of spirals

5) Mirror imaged rows of pattern 1

6) Vertical version of pattern 1

7) Alternate spiral pairs of pattern 6 mirror-imaged

8) Alternate groups of pattern 7 rotated through 90 degrees.

(Note the horizontal pairs have been moved apart so that the outer border edges are level.)

Leaf Borders

It has already been shown on page 34 that the leaf shape can be made into chain and cable borders. However, this is not the only border design that can be formed from this motif. Different arrangements offer other design possibilities.

Deeper borders can be formed by either vertical or diagonal placement of the leaf shape.

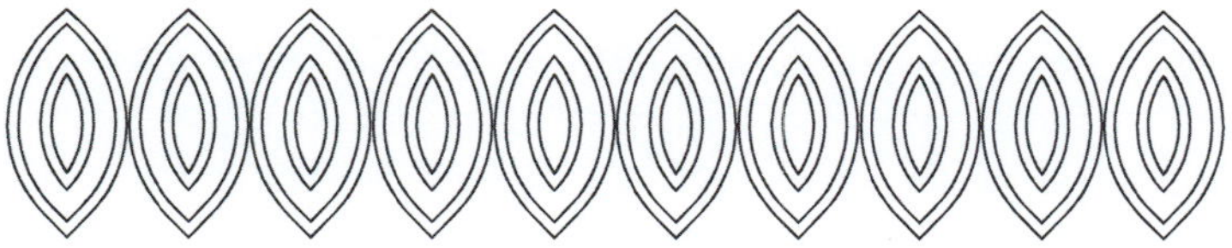

To adjust the length of a border, the motifs can be arranged to fit the space exactly by using the grid system previously described for the spiral border on page 35.

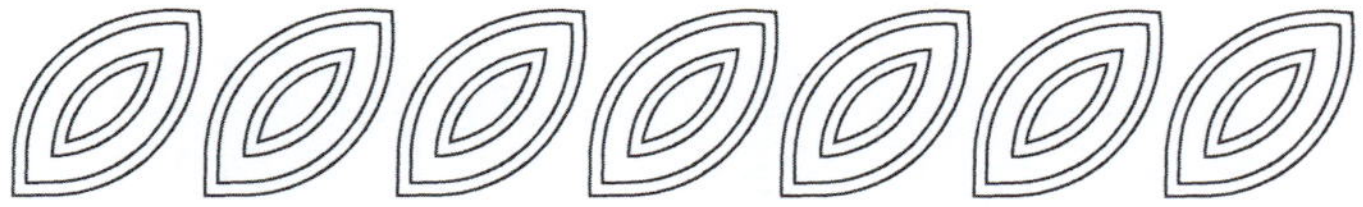

If alternate motifs are mirror-imaged using this diagonal placement, another border can be formed.

This border can also be mirror-imaged vertically to form a double border. The border will have symmetry if an even number of basic motifs are repeated and can be centred in two different ways.

Most borders on the previous page use the leaf rotated at an angle of 45 degrees. However, any angle may be used to make a border the required length.

(Note it is easier to omit the outer echo lines during the design stage.)

A steeper angle may cause the motifs to overlap and form secondary patterns.

When the motif is placed at an acute angle, it may be necessary to omit internal echo lines.

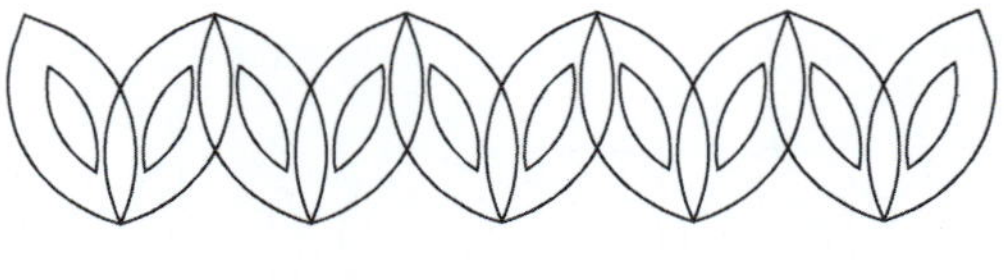

Whatever the final shape the leaf orientation makes, the outer edges should then be defined by a continuous echo line.

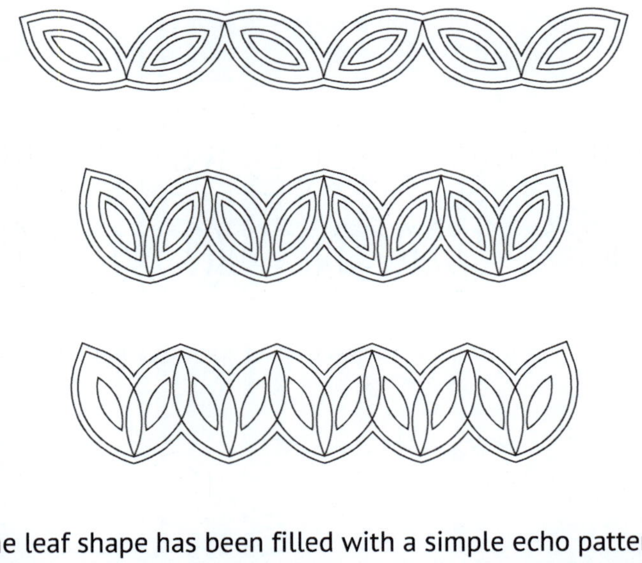

In these examples the leaf shape has been filled with a simple echo pattern. However, it is very important to remember that it can also be filled with a variety of other patterns (as shown on page 29).

Changing the filling of a motif can increase the design options enormously, although it is usual (but not a requirement) to attempt to maintain some continuity within a quilt design by not letting the patterns become overpoweringly 'busy'.

Not all leaf shapes are symmetrical. Bent leaf motifs can come in a variety of shapes and sizes, and can be used to create more sinuous borders.

As before, these motifs can be mirror-imaged into pairs. The angle of rotation will determine the depth of the border.

A paisley pear shape can be manipulated in the same way.

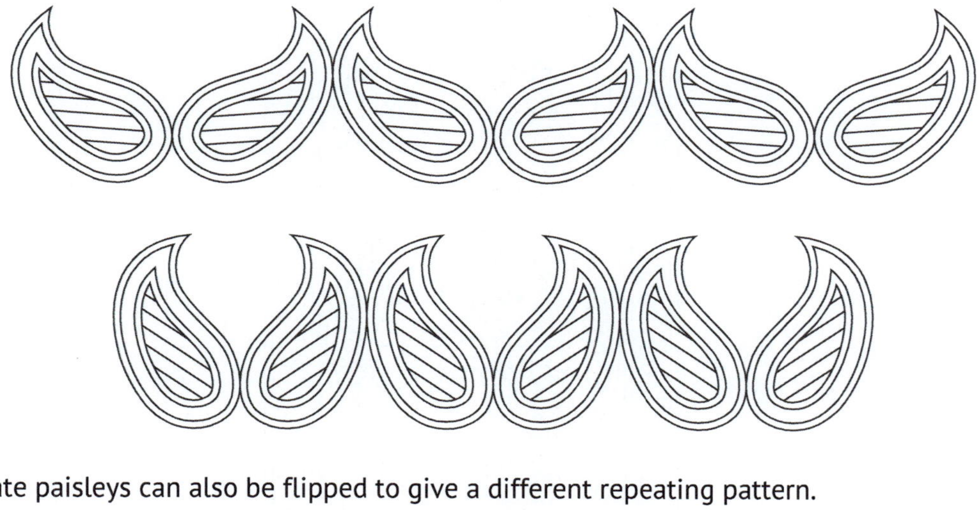

Alternate paisleys can also be flipped to give a different repeating pattern.

Both of these shapes can be embellished with small motifs such as a spiral or rose.

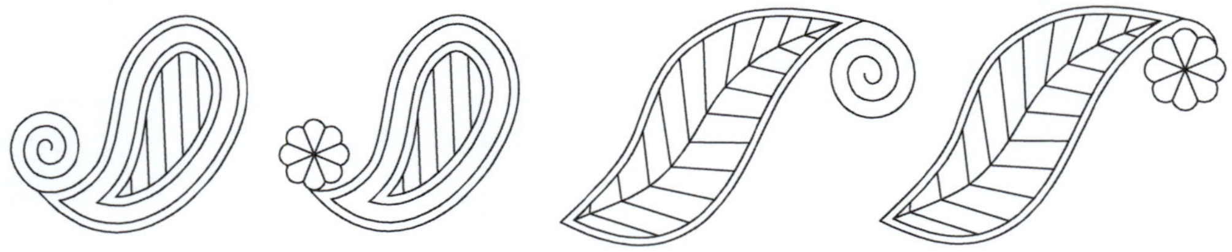

The rose or small leaf motif can also be added to a mirror-imaged bent leaf pair to form a flower border.

If the bent leaf shapes in the second border are flipped diagonally before the small leaf motif is inserted, it forms a tulip motif.

The resultant tulip shape can be filled and used as a border.

However, if this shape is reduced in size, it can replace the centre motif to form a tulip and bent leaf border.

Combining motifs is an excellent way of making larger, more complex borders!

Fans

Fans feature frequently in Welsh quilts. They may be scalloped, plain or pointed.

They are useful for filling corner spaces, but can also be arranged into borders and centrepieces.

Placed sideways in the same direction

Alternate fans flipped vertically

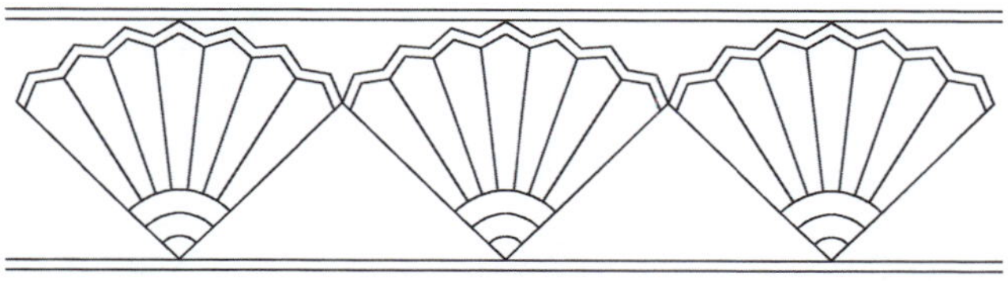

Placed facing vertically

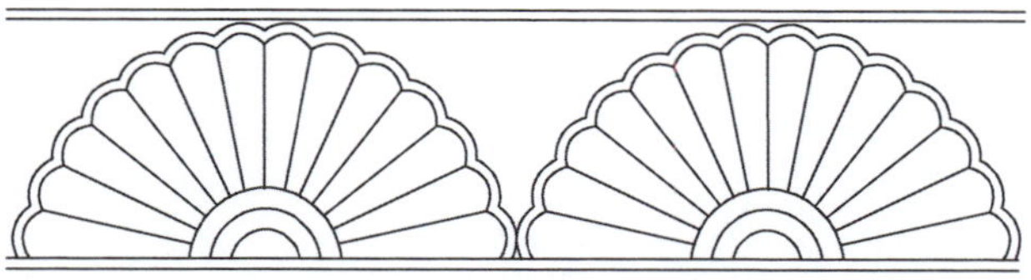

Mirror-imaged pairs in same direction

Alternate mirror-imaged pairs flipped vertically

Vertical and mirror-imaged

Welsh Squares

There are other more complex border designs traditional to Welsh quilts. One favourite is known as Welsh squares. The basic framework of this pattern divides the border into a series of squares on their points, with outer triangular filling spaces.

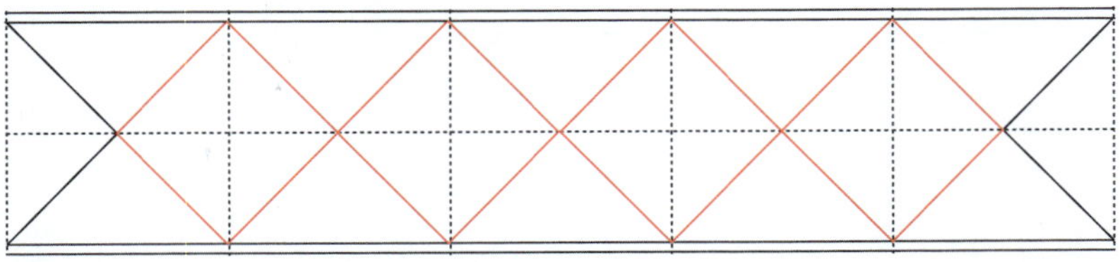

This pattern can be drafted to fit any space and frequently the 'squares' appear squashed and more diamond shaped.

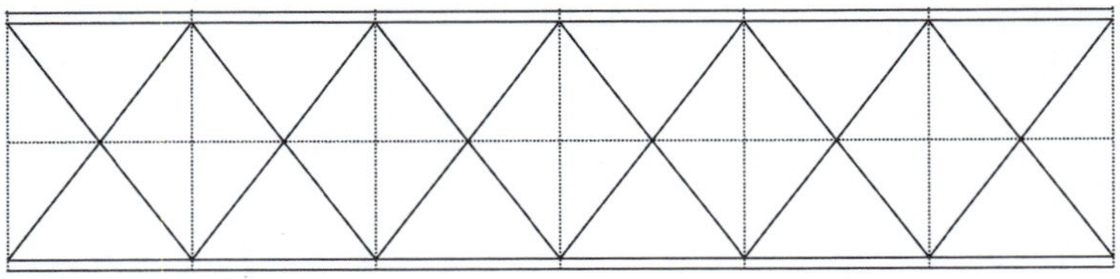

Welsh squares is an extremely versatile pattern which offers seemingly infinite design possibilities. The squares may be filled with a single repeating design, different designs or even background filling.

If the squares are filled with a motif, it is usual to then fill the triangles with a simple background pattern that acts as a counterpoint to the motif. This approach enhances the visual effect of the motif, allowing it to stand out rather than be overwhelmed by another pattern.

The background design can be varied in both style and position, and the dividing lines between the squares and outer triangles varied according to how the shapes are filled.

The traditional method for creating dividing lines is to echo the sides of each 'square' both inside and out. This gives a well-defined outline in which to place the motifs and background.

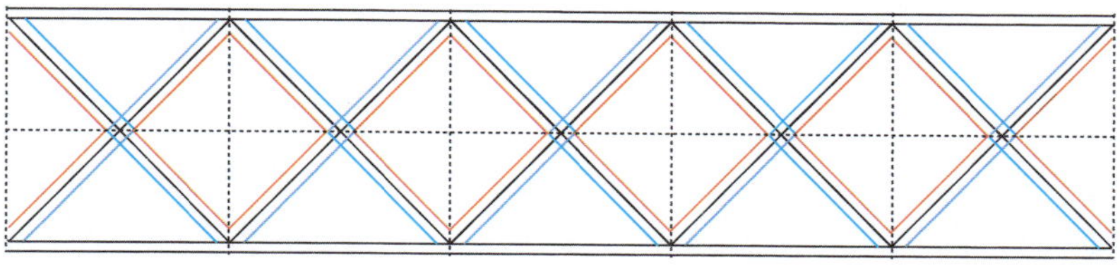

These are a few more examples of motifs that could be used to fill the squares.

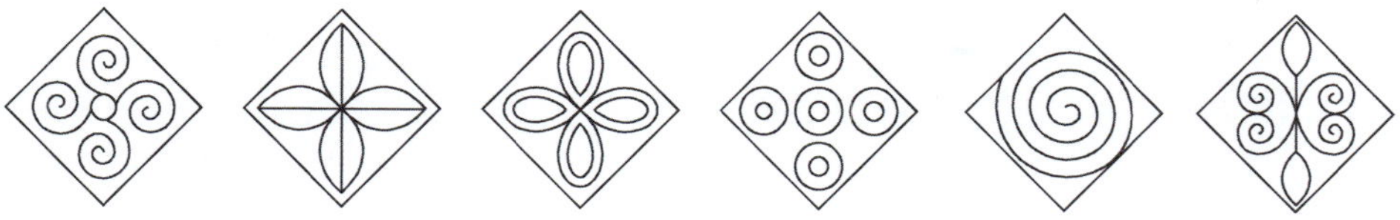

The opposite arrangement can also be used. The squares may be filled with a simple background pattern whilst the triangles contain the motif.

The triangles may be all the same...

...or have different motifs on opposite sides...

...or have an alternating arrangement.

By using only half the design, this particular version of Welsh squares is also useful for creating smaller borders.

Even more options are possible by varying the background designs. One or several background patterns can be used as illustrated here.

The simplicity of background patterns means they can be varied without overwhelming the impact of any motif(s) contained within the triangle shapes.

The design possibilities for Welsh squares are simply endless!

Church Window

Church window is another perennial favourite in Welsh quilt design. This tends to be a much larger pattern but offers the same multiple design options. (Effective use of both this and the Welsh squares border will be discussed in the *Using Borders That Turn Corners* section on page 96.)

The church window pattern is constructed from overlapping semi-circles, which again leave two distinct shapes to be filled.

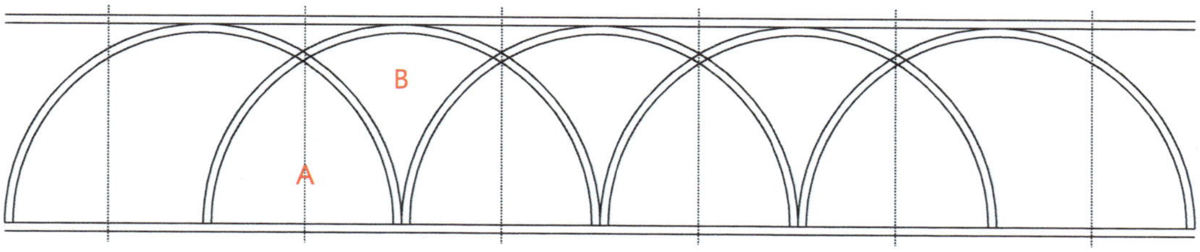

If the window shape (A) contains a motif, then the fan shape (B) is filled simply.

The reverse can also apply by placing the motif in the fan shape and keeping the window filling relatively simple.

Fillings can be alternated within these shapes. In this instance the fan shape filling has been alternated with a simple echo fill while the pattern within the window shape has remained constant.

Alternating or varying the motifs which fill the larger window shape yields many more design opportunities.

Finally, both areas can have alternating patterns - providing there is suitable contrast between them.

Given the number of different fillings available and the variety obtained by their placement, church window is extremely versatile. This is especially true on larger quilts where the pattern will be repeated multiple times.

Strippy Quilts

The simplest use of border patterns is in making strippy quilts. This type of quilt is versatile, easy to design and can be made to any size. It was a popular (and economical) way of using up fabric strips left over from making large plain wholecloth quilts.

Iâ Cnau Coco *Sandie Lush 2017*

The strips were generally 10-12" wide on large quilts and 5-6" on small quilts, but could vary in width both within a quilt and from quilt to quilt depending on its size.

Usually a quilt would be comprised of an odd number of strips in two colour-ways, giving symmetry to the finished quilt. However, in reality, quilts were made of any number of strips in whatever fabric came to hand.

It was never a hard and fast rule in Wales that the quilting patterns should follow the fabric strips. Many Welsh strippy quilts were quilted as if the quilt top was a single piece of fabric. Conversely, some Welsh quilts had quilting patterns which were arranged in strips but were actually stitched onto a single piece of fabric.

To illustrate strippy quilt design, it was decided to create a bent leaf and spiral motif border from the many patterns available.

Being asymmetrical in shape, this motif can be orientated in several directions to create a variety of border designs. Each orientation is shown in a different colour.

1) The motif can be arranged to run in a single direction the length of the strip.

2) Flipping alternate leaves provides a more sinuous strip design.

The leaves may also be mirror-imaged in a variety of ways to create interesting border designs.

3) A border may be mirror-imaged around its centre.

4) Mirror-imaging alternate leaves is another possibility.

5) Flipping alternate leaves in the above mirror-imaged pairs will yield another design.

6) Flipping alternate pairs in border 4 will create yet another design.

To act as a counterpoint to the intricate leaf and spiral strips, a cable design was chosen as the second border pattern.

The Welsh trail pattern originally shown on page 34 is deceptively simple. However, it is actually more complicated to draw than a regular under/over cable.

Its basic unit is a set of four equidistant and nested concentric leaf shapes.

When repeated as if to form a chain (a), the points of the outer (black) leaf shapes are each overlapped to rest against the point of the second (blue) leaf of the next set in the chain (b).

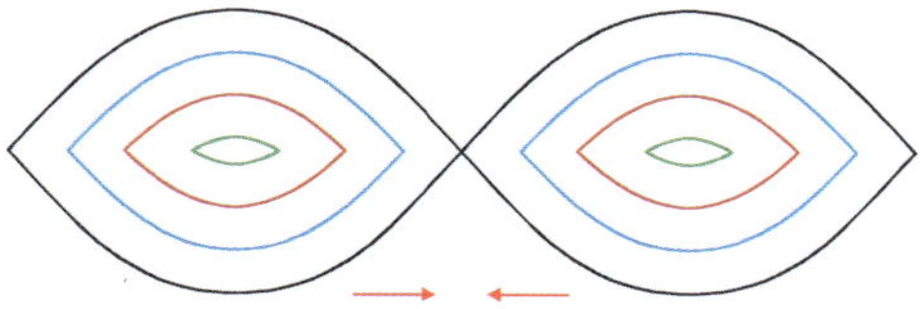
a

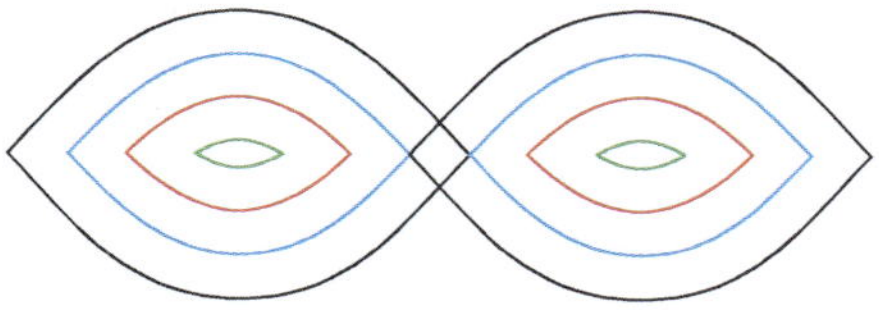
b

Next, the lines of the third (red) leaves are extended to echo the lines of the outer (black) leaves (c).

The same process is repeated for the inner (green) leaf, their lines being extended to echo the new red lines (d).

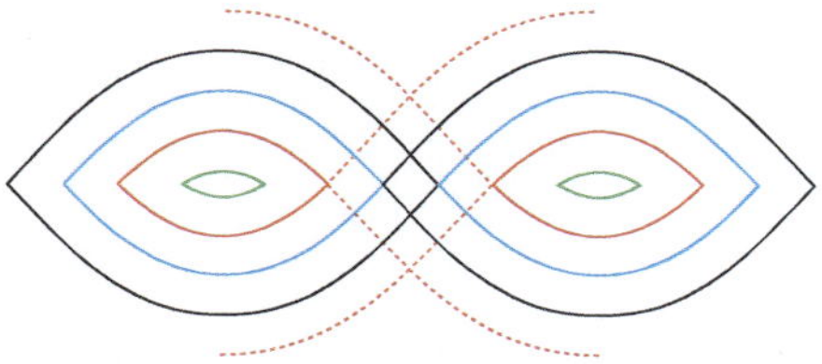
c

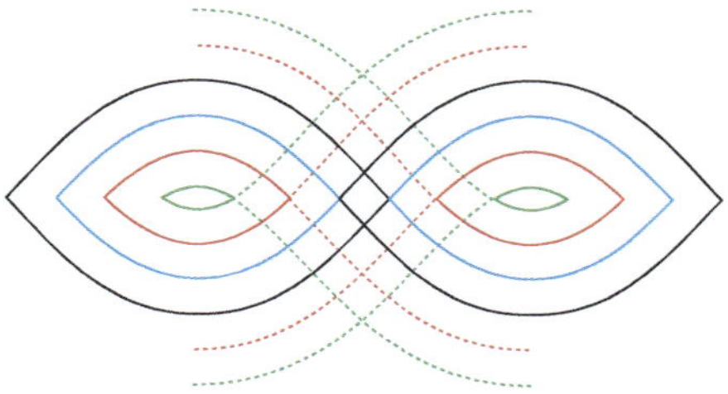
d

Where the extended green lines cross at a point beyond the cable defines the diamond shape. The outer (green) lines are erased beyond this meeting point (e).

The red lines are also erased where they extend beyond the diamond (f).

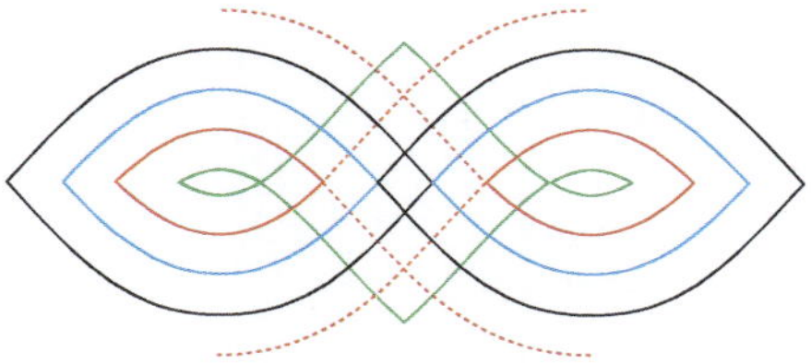
e

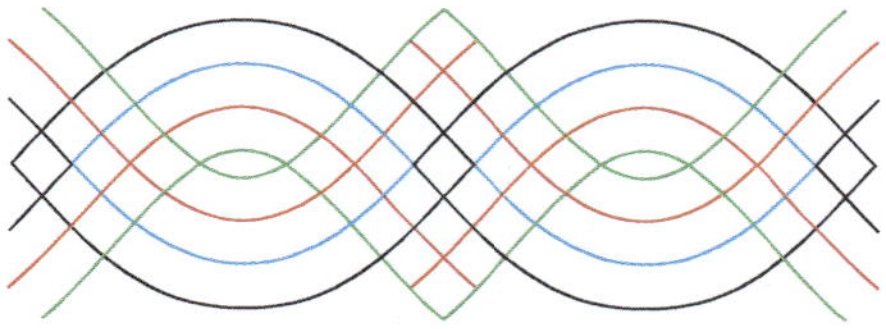
f

In previous times a quilter working on an old-fashioned frame would start the design at one end of a fabric strip and continue stitching until the other end of the strip was reached, regardless of how the pattern finished. These days a more precise approach is taken by starting the design in the middle of the strip to ensure symmetry around the centre.

Cables always have two possible central positions where this symmetry can be achieved; either at the widest part of the cable (A) or where the strands overlap (B).

A 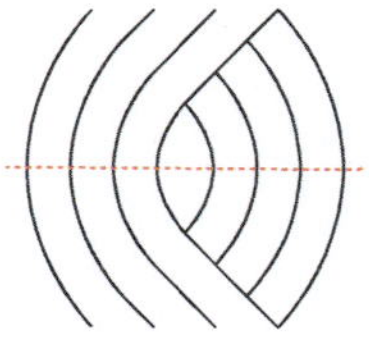

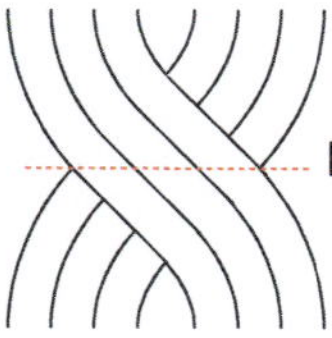 B

A 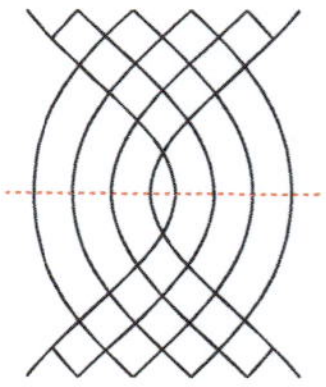

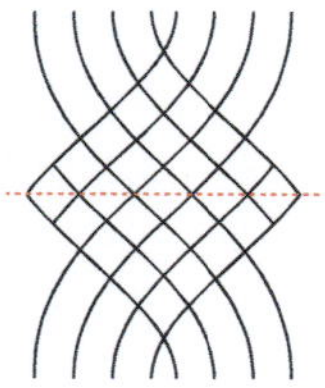 B

The design could start with each strip in the same central position (A, below).

When using an odd number of pattern strips, the central position of the middle cable may be shifted so that the cables alternate (B).

This second alternative will give more movement to the design while retaining symmetry across the quilt.

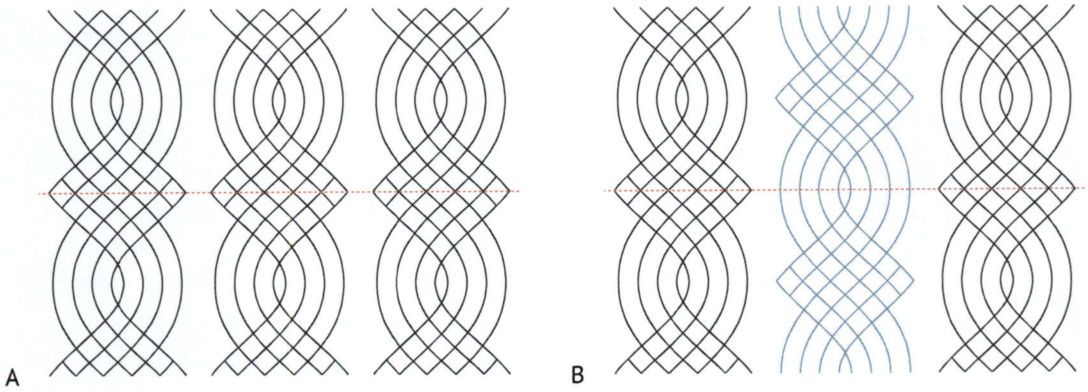

Using two designs in a strippy quilt with an uneven number of strips offers the potential to vary not only how the patterns are placed within the strips, but also which pattern is used as the predominant design.

Positioning the leaf and spiral pattern as the main design will give one set of options.

Although placing each leaf strip in the same direction is the simplest option, inverting the centre strip will give added movement to the design.

1) Quilt with middle leaf and spiral strip travelling in the reverse direction and Welsh trail centred on the diamonds.

Although the horizontal orientation of some leaves has changed in quilt 2 compared to quilt 1, the leaves within an individual strip travel in the same vertical direction in both designs.

2) Quilt 1 with alternate leaf and spiral motifs flipped horizontally.

By changing their vertical orientation, leaves can be arranged into pairs in a variety of ways to offer further design possibilities.

3) Quilt 1 with alternate leaf and spiral motifs flipped vertically.

Using the leaf as the secondary design will give a different set of options. These motifs are now positioned either side of the central strip, giving the opportunity to mirror-image them around it.

4) Motifs with downward-pointing spirals facing each other around the central strip.

The lower three leaf and spiral motifs could be flipped vertically to face up towards the centre.

All the designs so far have had the Welsh trail panels placed in the same way. Staggering their placement (as shown on page 50) can give more movement to the design.

5) Quilt 4 with the three upper leaf motifs flipped vertically at the centre.

The outer cables have been staggered leaving the diamond section of the middle cable to act as a central focus to the quilt.

Having the Welsh trail pattern centred on the diamond section of the motif tends to give the design a greater central focus. However, it is equally valid to centre the design on the plainer cable part of the motif.

It can be advantageous to have the spirals lie next to this part of the Welsh trail so that major design elements of each motif are shown to best effect rather than 'fighting' each other.

6) When the leaves are placed with spirals facing inwards, the middle Welsh trail strip is better placed centred on the cable part of the design with the outer panels centred on the diamond. The spirals then frame the plainest part of the Welsh trail motif.

7) When the leaves are placed with the spirals facing outwards, the reverse is true. Now the outer strips are centred on the cable and the middle strip is centred on the diamond. Again, this places the most patterned part of one motif against the plainest part of the other.

The addition of a third simple motif, for example a fan, will expand the range of design possibilities.

Now there is not only a greater choice of how the motifs are arranged within the strip, but also in the arrangement of the strips themselves.

Empty spaces around the motifs need filling with background quilting. Placement of motifs as well as the choice of background quilting patterns will increase the variation possible.

This quilt is shown on page 56.

Only three border patterns have been used here, but they could yield many more designs. With a wealth of patterns and fillings to choose from it can be seen that, although simple, the strippy format is incredibly versatile.

Designing and stitching the pattern to match the fabric strips would very much be regarded as 'English' in style and is illustrated by the quilt on page 151.

It is more likely a Welsh strippy using this format would appear like the reverse of that quilt (shown below). Although composed of five pattern strips it has been stitched on only three strips of fabric. It is this mismatch of style that gives Welsh quilts a reputation for being 'quirky'.

Dawns Ffan (reverse) *Sandie Lush 2017*

Unusual as the previous quilt may appear, there is still some correlation between the pattern and fabric as both are placed in strips. However, the most prevalent style of strippy quilt made in Wales would look like the quilt below.

In this typical Welsh strippy, made using exactly the same motifs, pattern placement totally disregards the position of the fabric strips. A pattern diagram for this quilt can be seen on the next page.

Gwanwyn (reverse) *Sandie Lush 2018*

This more intricate design format is the preferred Welsh quilting style. How these patterns are constructed and arranged will be explained in the following chapters.

The wholecloth side of this quilt is shown opposite.

Traditional Welsh Wholecloth Designs

Gwanwyn *Sandie Lush 2018*

Although many old quilts are based on a grid pattern or strippy format, the predominant style of Welsh quilt design follows the old-fashioned traditional British arrangement of a central medallion surrounded by a series of borders as shown in the diagram opposite.

This medallion style features in most old Welsh quilts. It was used regardless of whether the quilts were made from a single piece of fabric (wholecloth), simple or intricately pieced patchwork, or strips joined in the strippy format. It is this approach that makes makes Welsh quilts so distinctive.

Square Quilts

The design process for this traditional style of Welsh quilt is more complex than that for grid or strippy quilts. The patterns are now arranged as a series of borders around a collection of motifs which form a medallion. It is therefore essential to examine how the medallion designs are formed.

Usually, the central medallion echoes the shape of the finished quilt. Square quilts lend themselves to symmetrical designs and are therefore easier to construct, whereas single bed and cot designs are rectangular in shape and inherently more complex (how these are designed will be covered starting on page 108).

Fantasy (centre detail) *Sandie Lush 2004*

As circular designs sit harmoniously within a square shape, bed quilts and other square designs frequently have circular central medallions.

These can be created from a simple repeating motif, a series of motifs designed using the grid system, or something more complex such as a motif surrounded by a cable or spiral border.

Central Motifs for Square Quilts

The paper-cutting method described on pages 10-11 can be used with a large square of thin or tracing paper to create flowers with 16 or even 32 petals. The extra petals are made by further folding the paper before cutting or drawing the outer petal shape.

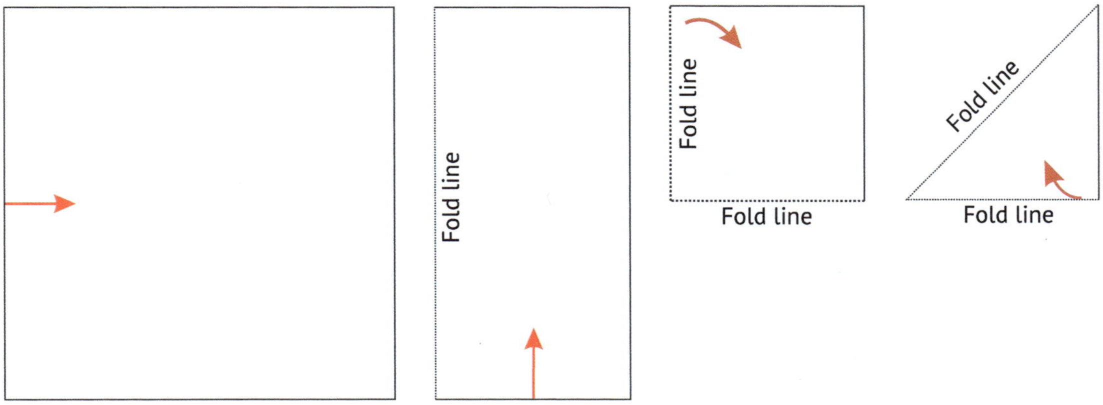

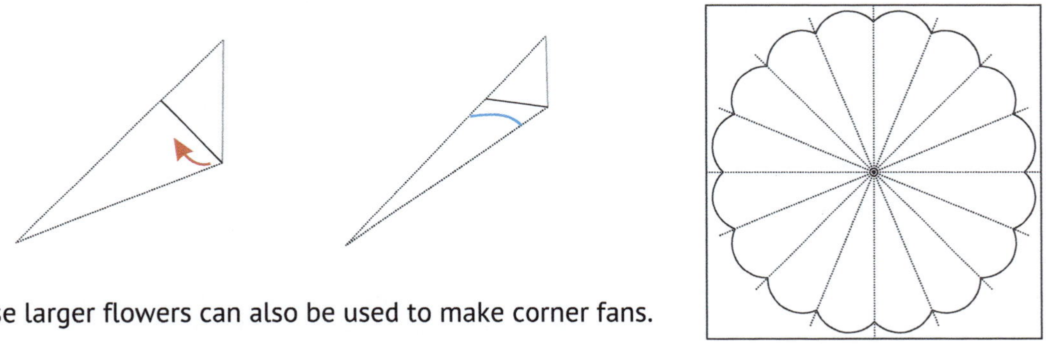

These larger flowers can also be used to make corner fans.

Cutting or drawing the outer outer edges with straight lines rather than in a curve will produce star shapes.

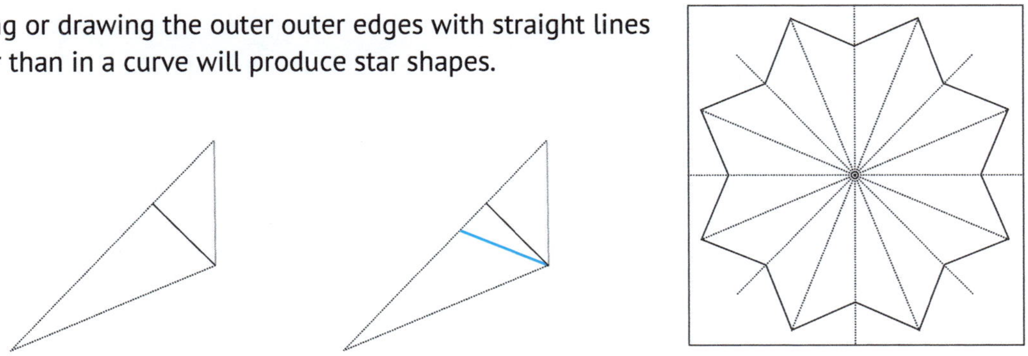

The number of folds will determine the number of points.

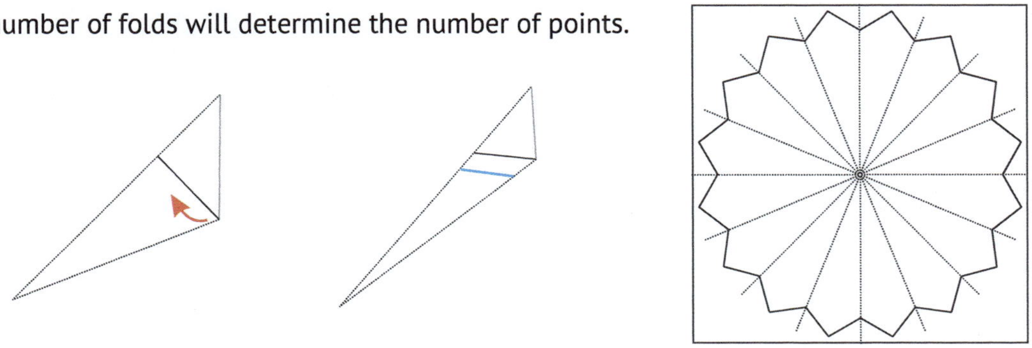

These motifs can also be created by first drawing a circle either with compasses or by tracing around a circular shape such as a dinner plate. The 'petals' can then be positioned using a protractor.
This gives greater flexibility to the number of petals formed. Rotating a line through the centre by 15 degrees will give 24 petals and when rotated by 20 degrees will give 18 petals.

Curved petal tops can then be drawn around cotton reels, coins etc. Regardless of the number of petals in the motif, it is usual to fill the centre to avoid having to stitch all the lines that meet there.
It is also usual to define the shape with an outer echo line.

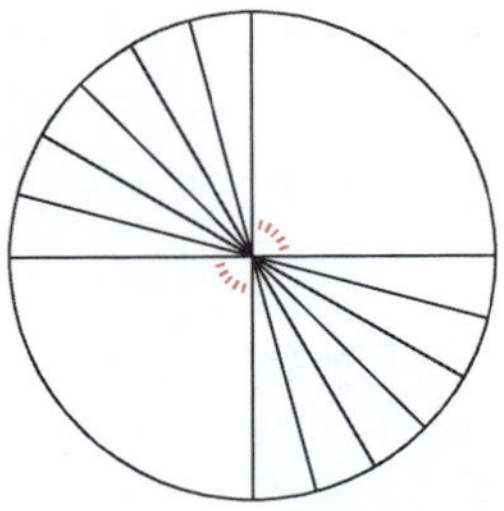

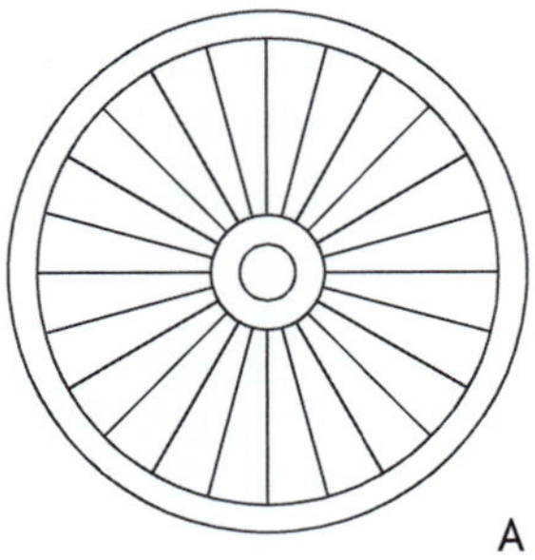

A

The plainer design (A) can be made more visually interesting by the addition of a border. This could be a chain constructed out of small leaf shapes or a series of spirals. Correct placement of these additional motifs can be achieved by temporarily extending the inner spokes of the wheel. These are then removed once the border has been constructed.

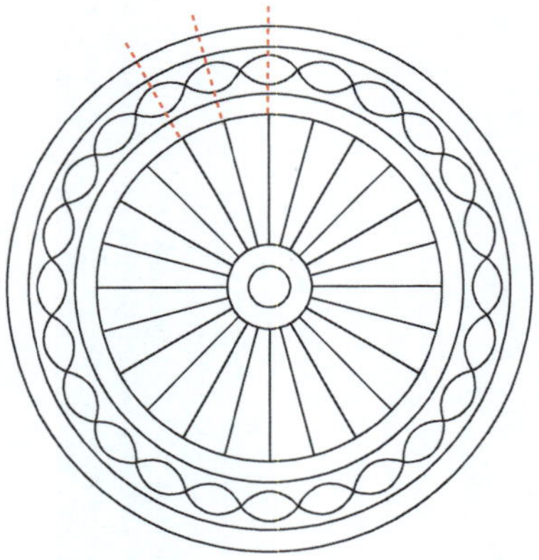

When the wheel spokes are spaced further apart, patterns can be inserted between them.

There are several ways in which a symmetrical leaf motif can be manipulated to produce circular designs.

Using a grid of four squares, simple rotation of the leaf within the grid can yield a circular shape. Although the four leaves are identical, the way they are rotated once they are filled can lead to several design options.

When filled with veins, the differences are minor but can alter the way a design flows within a finished quilt.

Leaf tips meeting horizontally

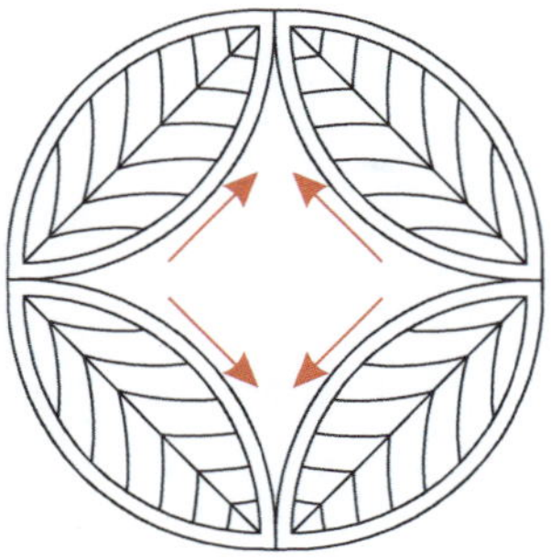

Leaf tips meeting vertically

Leaf tips rotating clockwise

Leaf tips rotating anticlockwise

When filled with an asymmetrical pattern, this effect becomes more pronounced.

Spiral ends meeting horizontally

Spiral ends meeting vertically

Spiral ends rotating clockwise

Spiral ends rotating anticlockwise

Some motifs can be rotated around a central point in more complex ways.

Rotating a leaf point by 45 degree increments will give a totally symmetrical eight-fold repeat.

This shape can be achieved by drawing around a simple leaf template.

The guidelines for placing the leaf motif can be created in two ways.

The simplest method is to carefully fold a square piece of paper into quarters and then across the diagonals to give an eight-fold repeat line. Alternatively, guidelines can be drawn using a pencil and ruler.

A motif can then be correctly placed on the crease lines to give a fully symmetrical design.

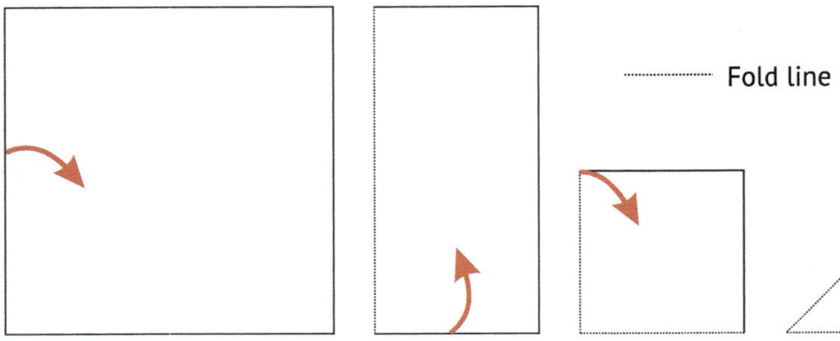

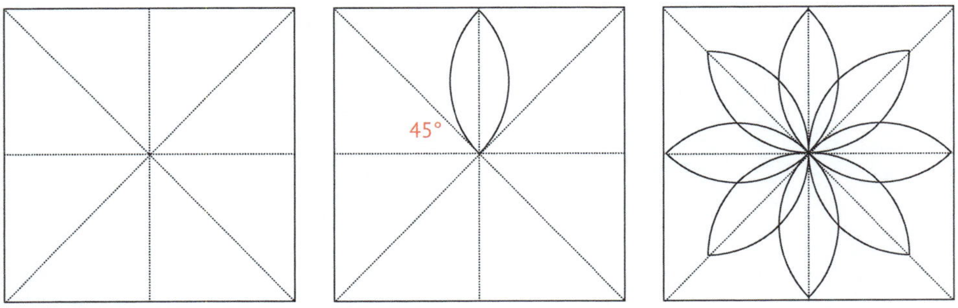

It is interesting to note that changing the width of the leaf motif used will alter the areas that require filling and will therefore affect the overall design.

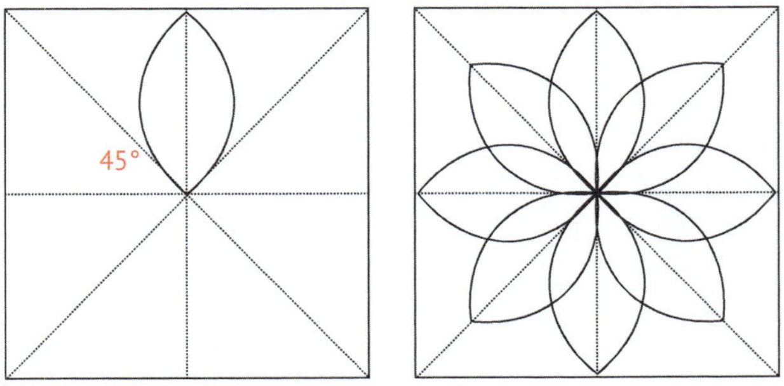

The traditional way to create central leaf motifs was simply to draw around circular household items such as saucers and tea or dinner plates. This allowed a variety of different sized motifs to be drawn directly onto a quilt in the frame using guidelines of chalked string.

This approach can also be used on paper. Guidelines are created as shown on the previous page and the household item lined up on these guides and drawn around to create overlapping circles.

Overlapping circles result in a more complex shape which can be used whole or pared down to a smaller design.

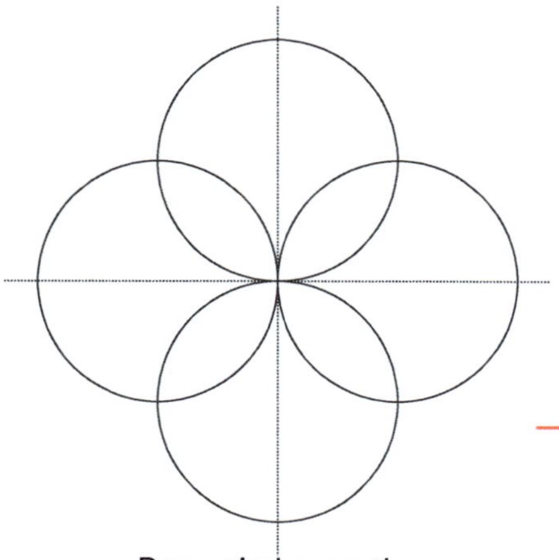

Draw circles on the vertical guides

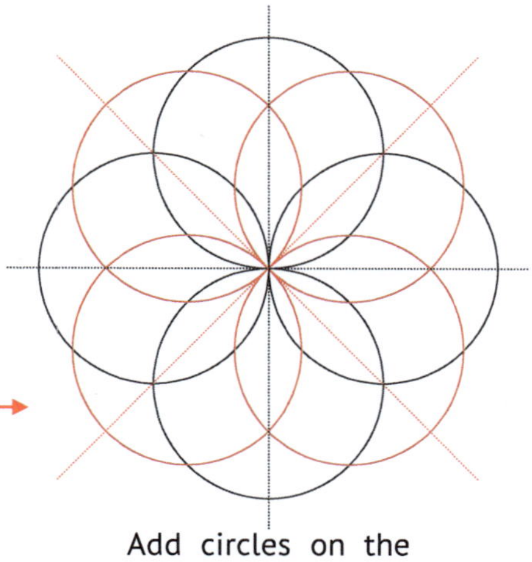

Add circles on the diagonal guides

Remove outer curves to give 'petal' shapes

The new outer curves can also be removed

Custom fill the remaining shapes and add an outer echo line.

The number of repeats and how they overlap will define the spaces that need filling.

The motifs on pages 64 and 65 have been filled with veins to give a naturalistic appearance, but other fillings can also be used.

Probably the most famous original Welsh central leaf design was created by Katy Lewis and is named the Abertridwr Star after the South Wales village in which she lived.

The following diagrams show how this distinctive motif is created.

An asymmetrical shape such as a paisley pear offers even greater design possibilities.

The motif can be rotated in 60 degrees steps around the centre to give a symmetrical six-fold repeat. This will result in slightly elongated shapes which are often used in smaller and rectangular quilts (these are discussed in greater detail starting on page 108).

The main vertical focus of the resultant design can be determined by the placement of either the spirals (A) or the paisley shape (B).

A

B

Varying the initial orientation of the motif can give more unusual designs.

The motifs can rotate in either a clockwise (A) or anti-clockwise (B) fashion.

A

B

An eight-fold repeat of the motif will give larger designs suitable for bed quilts.

The motif is rotated in 45 degree steps around the centre and can be placed with the spirals either inward or outward facing.

Again, the angle at which the motif is initially placed will determine the overall size and shape of the centrepiece.

circular

square

All of these medallions will require the addition of other quilting patterns to fill the space.

Smaller spaces created by repeating motifs can be occupied by fillers such as circles.

Spaces may also be filled with background quilting patterns such as echoes or lines.

Some designs leave larger spaces to be filled. However, simply filling a large area with background quilting does not give the finished quilt a central focus (A).

A B C

The addition of the smaller leaf motif (B) creates a central focus, but the combination of paisley, leaf and background fillings provides too much variety and the overall effect is a lack of harmony.

A centrepiece such as that shown in version C is more sympathetic to the paisley motif. This version not only has more visual impact, but also provides a sense of movement to the finished design.

Many of the cushion examples from the section on the grid system (pages 14-16 and 22-23) may be used whole or in part for the centre of a quilt.

For example, the grid system was used to orientate the leaf motif into either a centre circle or a cross. This was then surrounded by a border containing other simple motifs (A&D).

Removing the border and then simply rotating motifs around the central circular cluster can yield both square and circular shapes (B&C).

A

B

C

Inserting motifs into spaces between those in a central cross can create new designs (E&F).

D

E

F

As shown on the previous page, rotating motifs such as the leaf or paisley around a centre point can leave a large central space to be filled.
Conversely, when using the above approach, the centrepiece designs created can be relatively compact and may need to be extended to a suitable size.

Small circular designs can be enlarged by the addition of an extra border(s). These should be enclosed in a double tramline to give the pattern greater definition.

Enlarging square designs into suitably sized centrepieces can be slightly more complex. The outer confines of the square could be increased in size, but the addition of extra filler patterns may not actually enhance the design. In fact, the central pattern may easily become lost in a sea of background quilting (A).

A more effective way to extend a square design is to rotate it by 45 degrees and set it into a larger square (B).

A

B

This will create corner spaces which can be filled with another motif such as a fan.

The original 'box' can then be removed and the remaining space filled with a background filling pattern.

ASSEMBLING THE MOTIFS INTO A QUILT

Armed with the knowledge of how to create borders and motifs and use them to create larger designs, along with a selection of background quilting patterns, it is now possible to create a traditional Welsh wholecloth quilt design.

This form of design may initially appear more daunting to tackle, but it simply uses a combination of the techniques previously described for designing quilts by the grid and strippy methods.

The first step is to choose a design to place in the centre of the quilt.

The centre can be formed from a single motif which has been rotated to overlap.

It can also be formed from a combination of smaller motifs arranged into a square design.

Smaller designs can be surrounded by further borders to make larger centrepieces.

The next step is to draw a double tramline to define the size of the square in which the centrepiece will sit. This can be exactly the same size as the outer edges of the centrepiece (A&B), or it can occupy a larger space (C).

A

B

C

If the central motif is circular, it will be necessary to fill the empty spaces in the corners of the square. The fan shape is a popular motif for filling larger spaces. Flowers, hearts, spirals and any variety of background fillings provide a wealth of options for smaller spaces.

With so many possibilities available, it can sometimes be useful to leave these smaller spaces empty at this stage. As the design progresses, other motifs used elsewhere may prove to be suitable fillers. This approach can help give the finished design harmony rather than it becoming a busy mix of different styles.

Once the central design has been set, the ends of the tramlines are extended. By doing this, the next spaces to be filled become more obvious with the area surrounding the centre now forming an open border on each side with an open box at each corner.

1/10th scale

Historically, corner boxes were very important in Welsh quilt design. Filling these boxes with a pattern unrelated to the adjacent border removed the necessity of finding designs that not only fitted the required shape, but also turned the corners in a pleasing or symmetrical fashion. It also meant quilters did not need the mathematical skills required to create such continuous designs.

The border area is worked first as the width of the pattern chosen will determine the size of the corner boxes. For this quilt the first Welsh squares border from page 42 is used.

Having chosen a pattern, it is usual to centre it around the mid-line of the quilt so that the border ends are symmetrical.
Most border patterns will have a choice of two points around which the centre can be based.

To help visualise its best placement, it can be useful to trace a length of border design longer than required and line up the various centre border options.

A

B

In example A, the motif element of the border has been placed in the centre. This arrangement leaves slightly less than half a motif at either end of the border where it meets the tramlines.

In example B, the filled outer triangle element of the design has been placed in the centre. This provides a better solution for two reasons:-

Firstly, two complete pattern repeats are utilised which gives greater focus to the motif than to the background fill.

Secondly, the diagonal filling lines at either end can be finished at any point along their length. Not having a full repeat does not detract from their impact.

Having chosen option B, all four side borders can be filled.

The inner tramlines can now be trimmed to their correct size. The corner boxes have now been defined.

The corner boxes can now be filled with either a motif, a background pattern or both.

Very occasionally, the mathematics work out (as shown below) and the border can travel completely around the quilt. In these cases, the boxes can be removed.

However, the version of the design below lacks the visual impact of the one above.

It is also easier to treat the corners as separate entities than attempt to make a border fit perfectly!

Once the first border design is set, its outer tramlines can be extended. These become the inner tramlines of the second border and define the next areas to be filled.

With the inner tramlines of the next border in place, another border pattern now needs to be chosen.

If the border is made up of motifs, these can be placed accurately by dividing the border into an appropriate number of equal spaces with markers (1).

Some motifs can be adapted to fit a space. Others, such as leaf and heart shapes, can be custom made to fit (2). This is achieved by folding and cutting a piece of paper to exactly the required size as described on page 10.

Once the new border is in place, any temporary markers can be removed and the outer tramlines added (3). This will create the corner boxes (4) which can be filled with either new design elements or ones which continue the theme set by existing motifs.

Any remaining empty spaces within each border and box should be filled with echo or background quilting. As all other motifs are outlined, an inner tramline has been added to the 'square' element of the Welsh squares borders to give continuity of design (5).

If the central space was left unfilled, now is the time to fill this space with a small motif or background filling.

A

1/15th scale

So far only echo and straight line fillings have been used in this design. Either of these can be used to fill the centre space.

The differences can be subtle: the echo quilting in version A gives a sense of movement whereas the straight lines in version B become continuous with the lines in the next border, making a secondary pattern. Both are effective and either could be used in the centre.

B

Any sized quilt design can be built up in this fashion and it is amazing how quickly a design can grow.

Traditional Welsh quilt designs are generally a central medallion surrounded by three borders which tend to get larger towards the outer edge of the quilt. However, part of the beauty of Welsh quilts is the absence of set design rules, so the number and size of borders used is purely the choice of the designer.

The number and types of borders selected will also depend on the required finished size of the quilt.

The final border chosen for this example was created from large spirals.

The spiral can be manipulated to form a continuous border using the grid system (as shown on page 35).

The addition of an outer border of spirals confers a finished look to the design but does not greatly increase the finished size of this design. Should a larger design be required, the quilt can be expanded by the addition of extra border(s).

In the example below, two extra borders have been added.

To act as a counterpoint to the existing inner leaf border, the leaf motif was used in a different orientation in the new outer border. It was placed to travel clockwise around the quilt to match the orientation of the previous spiral border.
The corner boxes were filled with a smaller version of the spiral motif in the Welsh squares rotated by 45 degrees.

Finally, this second leaf border was enclosed by another continuous spiral border to complete the design.

Keeping the orientation of the spirals the same in both borders gives the finished design a sense of flow.

The design can also be expanded by choosing a wider pattern for one of the outer borders. The one illustrated below was created using the grid system with a heart motif. The corner boxes were filled with the central four leaf motif.

A small spiral border was added to finish the design. This echoes the spiral border which surrounds the central four leaves and gives a sense of continuity to the finished quilt, as does the use of the central concentric circles at the corners of this border.

This quilt is shown opposite.

Exploring different fillings for both the corner spaces and the motifs will lead to many alternative design options.

Two of the many possible variations are shown on page 82.

Version A features new fillings for both the leaf and heart motifs.

Version B has a new Welsh squares filling (without the additional tramline within the 'square' added on page 76). This version also has an alternative design within the heart motifs and a different design approach for the outer corner boxes of that border.

Rhew Glas *Sandie Lush 2017*

In A, the leaf motif has been filled with petals. As a counterpoint, the hearts have been filled with straight lines similar to the leaf veins in the original design.

A

In B, a new spiral and contour design within the heart motifs echoes the new Welsh square filling. Additionally, the four-heart motif created for the third border is also used in that border's corner boxes, making it continuous around the quilt.

B

There is usually more than one way to achieve something, and Welsh quilt design is no exception!

For the quilts in the previous section, filling the centre space was guided by the patterns selected for the surrounding borders. An equally valid approach would be to fill the centre spaces at the outset.

With this alternative approach, those initial decisions will guide subsequent choices. While this strategy helps limit the number of decisions to be made at a later stage, the range of patterns available can make getting started more difficult.

Here are the same three centre options from page 72. This time, once defined by tramlines, the empty spaces around the motif are filled before the addition of any borders.

A

B

C

It is usual to make the filling act as a counterpoint to the main design.

For example the straight lines in the leaf fill in version A are best offset by a background containing some curved elements.

Conversely, the circular designs of version B would be shown to best effect by a background made of straight lines.

If the central space has been enlarged, as in version C, a mixture of both curved and straight designs will most effectively fill the space.

A circular fill will echo the centre motif and provides movement to the design.

However, the use of a straight line fill will act as a counterpoint to both the circular motif and the fans. This will result in a better central focus.

Extension of these designs into larger pieces follows exactly the same process as before; the tramlines are extended to create border and corner box spaces which are then filled.

The same basic quilt design from the previous example was used, but this time the starting point was to fill the centre spaces with a square diamond pattern as shown on page 84.

For continuity of design, the square diamond fill now needs to be used elsewhere. In this version it is used to fill the spaces around the fans in the corner boxes.

As before, the design can then be extended with additional borders into a square quilt.

It is important to ensure continuity of design. The corner box design incorporates the spiral fill (above) and the square diamond fill (below).

The corner boxes could also be filled with fans. Their orientation will offer different design outcomes.
They can be arranged to face in towards the centre or out towards the corners and can have the same or opposite orientation to those in the inner border.

How the fans are orientated also alters the appearance of a border. Inward facing fans accentuate the separate border areas, whereas outward pointing fans give these borders a sense of flow around the corners.

Other more obvious changes, such as substituting a different motif in the corner boxes or the addition of an extra border, all lead to a wealth of alternative designs.

Historically, many professional quilters adopted this strategy; by making various (often small) changes to a basic design, each version could then be sold as an 'original' pattern.

Using Small Borders to Divide Patterns

Tarian Aur (detail) *Sandie Lush 1999*

Using a small border rather than simple tramlines to divide the main patterns from each other adds complexity to a design.

For the following example a fan shape was chosen as the central motif.

This shape could be defined by an echo line around the outside (A) or it could be confined in a set of circular tramlines (B).

A B

Option B was chosen and set into a centre box.

The remaining spaces could be filled with echo (A) or background (B) quilting.

A

B

The space could also be filled with a small motif (C). This option was chosen for the following design example.

C

A small cable was chosen to act as a dividing border.

This could be centred in two ways to give symmetry at the corners.

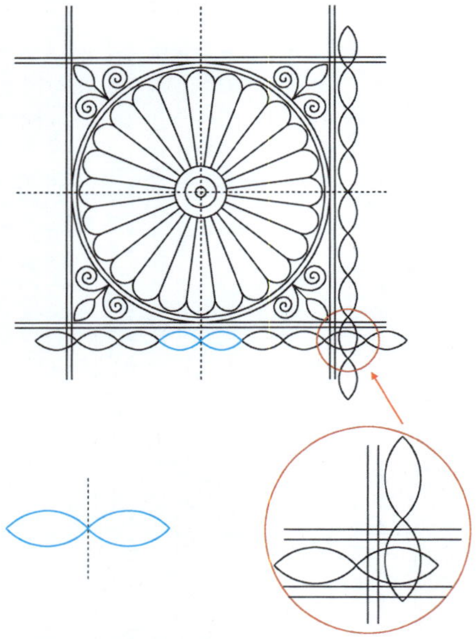

A) When centred on the joins, the cables overlap at the corner.

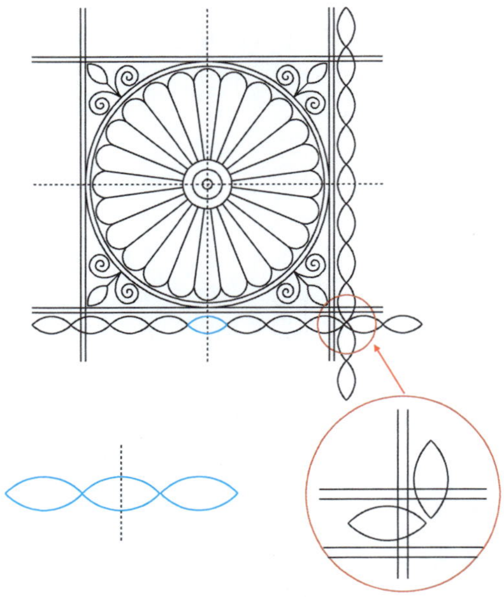

B) When centred on the leaf, the cables almost meet at the corner.

Option B is a better fit, but neither option precisely matches at the corner. This can be addressed in several ways.

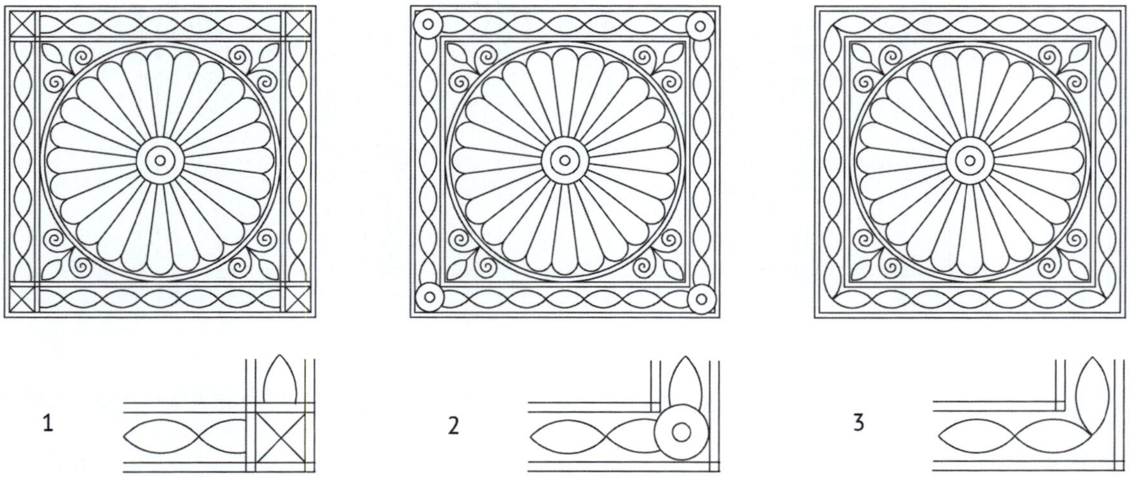

1) The cable can be cropped at the tramlines and a new motif or shape introduced into the corner box.

2) A small motif or shape can be used to cover (and therefore hide) the gap where the cables do not quite meet at the corners.

3) The cable can be resized by dividing the border space into equal boxes and then paper-cutting a new leaf shape to fit. This approach is the most time-consuming option.

Corner option 2 was chosen and used throughout this design to illustrate how small borders can be used to separate patterns in the same way tramlines did in earlier examples.

Each small border was created using the same process as described on the previous page. The circles were placed at the corners regardless of whether or not the end points of the cables met at the corners.

At this stage it was also decided that the fan motif used in creating the centrepiece would also be used for the outermost border of this design.

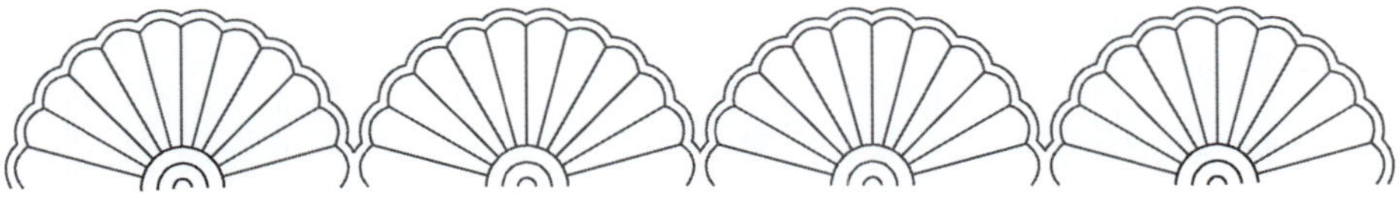

In an earlier example on page 75, a border could have been positioned to turn the corner seamlessly without the addition of a corner box. Although not desirable for that design, with some patterns this can confer continuity at the corners and give the design a sense of flow around the quilt.

By using strategy 3 on the previous page, this is relatively easy to achieve with smaller borders, but larger patterns such as fans or a church window border can prove problematic.

To achieve continuity in this design, it was easier to create and position the fan border next in the sequence despite it being the final border. If the quilt is to be a required size, it may still be necessary to slightly reduce the scale of the design.

Both inner and outer edges of the fans were then enclosed with the small cable border.

The spaces within this fan border were filled with the same small motif used in the centre.

The remaining border space could then be filled in a variety of ways.

Possibly the easiest solution was to divide the border into boxes which could be filled with motifs and/or background quilting.
In this design, the corner boxes are square but the boxes sub-dividing the border are slightly longer than they are wide.

An alternative solution was to divide the border space into a series of triangles.

These spaces were then filled with a variety of straight lines to offset the curved patterns of the fans and a slightly enlarged version of the petal and spiral motif used to fill the centre corner spaces.
The corner boxes were filled with a heart motif containing a diagonal line fill.

This quilt is shown opposite.

Having introduced the heart motif, alternative fillings could provide further design options. In the example below, a spiral fill was chosen. This new heart motif was then combined with the fan shape to give an alternative centre pattern.

Dadeni (reverse) *Sandie Lush 2017*

Using Borders That Turn Corners

Suo Gân (detail) *Sandie Lush 2009*

Probably the most spectacular border used in Welsh quilts is the church window.

Although this can simply be run in strips on a strippy quilt, it is most often used as a continuous border around the outer edges of large quilts.

While difficult to draft, the overlapping semi-circles provide ample opportunities for using different filling patterns (see pages 45-46).

As with borders made from fans (as used in the last example) or Welsh squares, church window borders can either be placed to run continuously around the corners, or separated with a corner box.

With fans and Welsh squares this is a relatively simple process, but church window corners are more complex.

Depending on the size of the finished quilt and how the border is centred, different corner designs will occur. The pattern can be centred in either of two positions within the border.

A

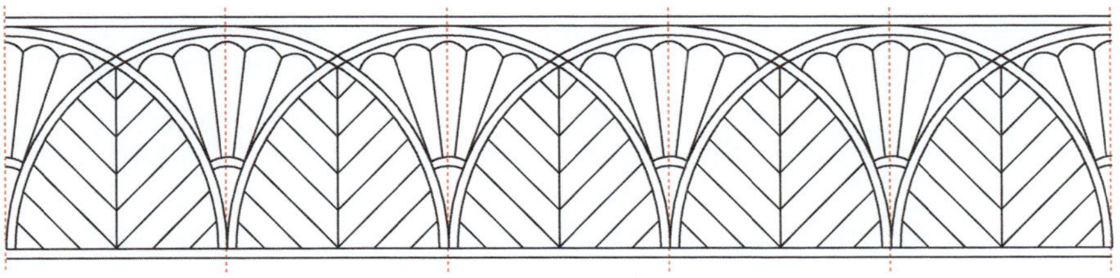

B

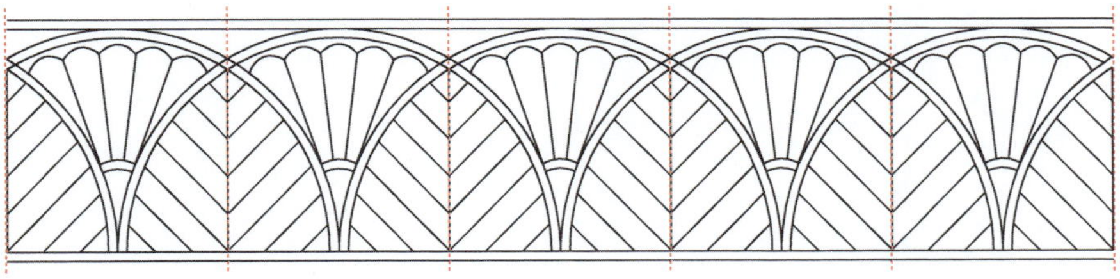

The simplest way to turn a corner is to extend the tramlines from adjacent borders to form corner boxes which can then be filled with other motifs.

How the border is centred will determine the pattern at the corners and therefore the motifs used to fill the boxes.

Placing a fan in the box would impart a sense of continuity of ideas but not of actual pattern.

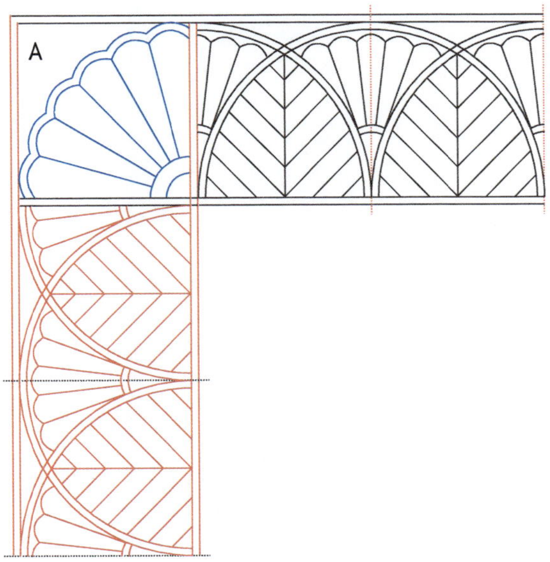

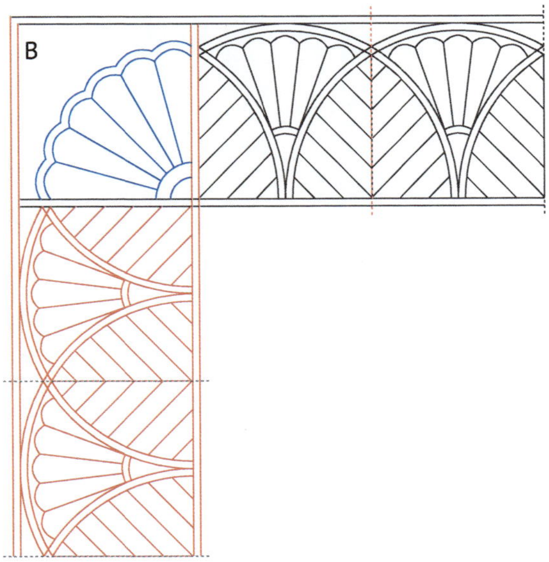

In the above example, the size of the fan had to be adapted to match the adjacent borders. The lack of similarity of scale between the corner fan and church window fans is less obvious in version B and provides better continuity of pattern.

However, version A imparts a better sense of flow.

Although the flow of the design may become disrupted, border B can be used to turn the corner in a continuous fashion within the corner box. The defining lines of this box can then be removed once the corner design is complete.

With this method, the half-leaf motif is not removed beyond the ends of the borders. When the tramlines from both borders are extended to create the box, it can be seen that the lines in the end leaf motifs overlap but do not exactly align with each other. However, if the position of the overlapping borders is adjusted so that these motif filling lines are aligned, a corner pattern can be produced and the internal lines of the box removed.

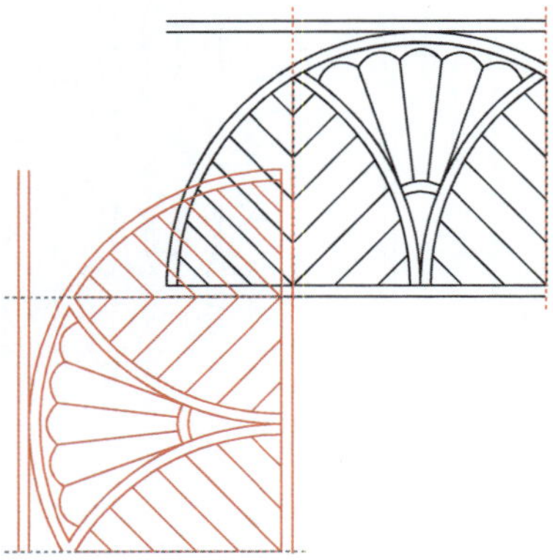

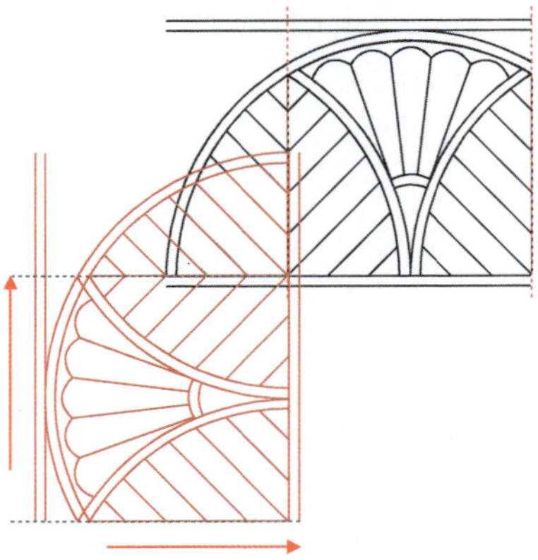

The leaf filling in this new corner shape could be aligned in different ways.

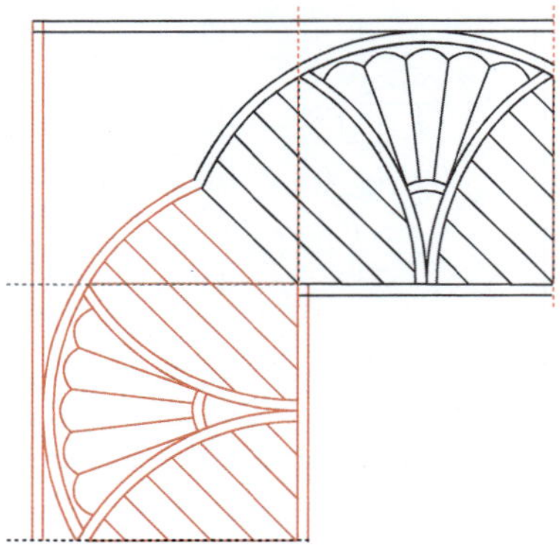

The corner space can then be filled. How this is achieved would depend on how the new corner shape was filled. The simplest solution would be to use an echo or background filling.

So far only the 'leaf' part of the church window has been extended out into the corner.

However, the 'fan' part of the border could also be extended and the overlapping patterns used to create the outer corner filling.

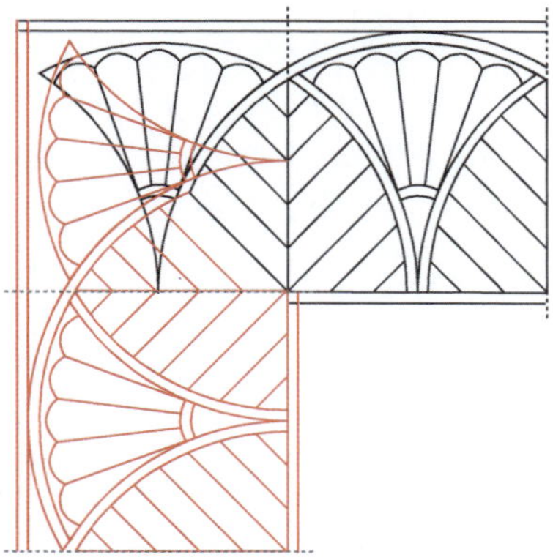

The addition of an extra fan to each border has the potential to give an interesting corner design.

After outlines have been removed the shape becomes clearer.

Placement of a diagonal guideline across the corner will indicate the centre point to which the fan lines will need adjusting. This is illustrated using half of the additional corner pattern.

Once one half of the corner is adjusted, a mirror image can be drawn to complete the design.

Whether pleasing corner motifs can be formed will very much depend of the fillings chosen in the two church window compartments.

In the past, great store was placed on the ability to create a truly continuous church window border which flowed in an uninterrupted fashion around a quilt. An experienced quilter would have known the length of the template and exactly how many repeats would be needed for a single or double bed-sized quilt. For example, using a 24" template there would be a 3 x 4 repeat for a single quilt and a 4 x 4 repeat for a double quilt.

Modern quilts are more flexible in size, and patterns are now adjusted to fit. When turning the corner in a continuous fashion, the simplest way to see all the options available is to have two lengths of the pattern drawn out.

The drawings need to be one repeat longer than half the total size of the border to be filled. In this way they may be overlapped to show where the optimal centre and corner position placements are located. This will also determine both the size of the border and the size of the finished quilt.

Traditionally, there are two main ways to turn the corner of a church window border in a continuous fashion.
Border A from page 97 produces an elongated leaf shape where the semi-circles of the borders overlap at the corner.

This shape can then be filled with veins to match the fillings already used, or another motif entirely.

Option A on page 97 can also create borders which overlap to form a circular shape in the corner by removing the 'leaf' element and replacing it with a fan.

Once the 'leaf' is removed, the remaining space can be filled with more 'petals' to form a continuous fan shape. Some adjustment may be necessary and the corner fan is best created on one half of the design and mirror-imaged across the corner (as illustrated on page 99).

Modern quilts can vary greatly in size, so it is useful to explore less rigid ways of turning the corner of a design.

One method is to adapt the pattern to fill the space and even extend beyond it. The designs below have been created using border B from page 97.

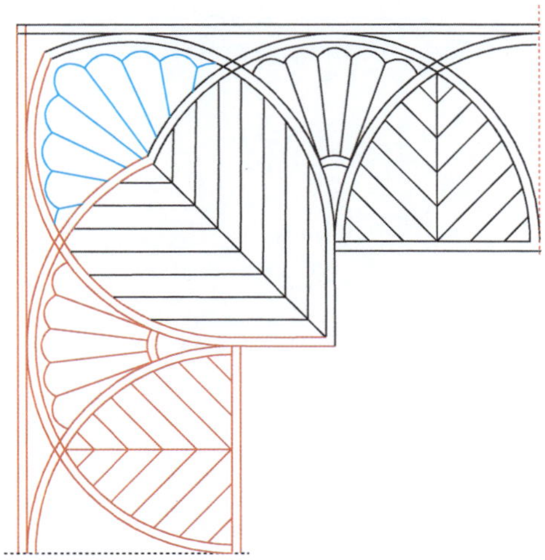

Nowadays, the easiest and most popular design approach for turning border corners is to use one or more mirror tiles. This will still impose certain size constraints on the quilt designs but gives a more flexible set of options.

When placed onto the border pattern at a 45 degree angle, the mirror tile makes the entire corner/border image visible. The mirror can be moved along the border until a pleasing corner is found.

Usually there is more than one possible outcome.

Once a position has been selected, a line can be drawn along the lower edge of the tile.

If the paper is then folded along that diagonal line, a mirror image can be traced to form the corner design.

By placing a second mirror tile at a 90 degree angle to the border design, this method can also be used to centre a border.

When viewing in a mirror or tracing along a fold, the direction of a pattern will be reversed.

Many symmetrical patterns such as the rose and fan will not be affected.

However, asymmetrical or directional designs such as the spiral can create an interesting change of direction in the centre of the border.

Unfortunately, this change of direction can prove problematic when turning corners.

Spiral borders are more effective when the design flows around a corner, but mirror-imaging at this point can interrupt the flow of a design (A).

It is better to mark the positions of the spirals with circles rather than trace the motif itself (B).

A

B

The circles can later be used as placement guidelines when tracing the spirals in their correct orientation. A corner spiral may need repositioning slightly so that it aligns neatly with both borders (B).

C

If this adjusted quarter design (C) is subsequently rotated around the quilt centre rather than mirror-imaged, the spirals will flow continuously around the quilt.

Cable designs also pose interesting problems when creating a continuous border rather than one separated by corner boxes. A mirror tile can again be used to find pleasing places to turn the corner.

However, the under/over sequence of a cable is disrupted when it is mirror-imaged.

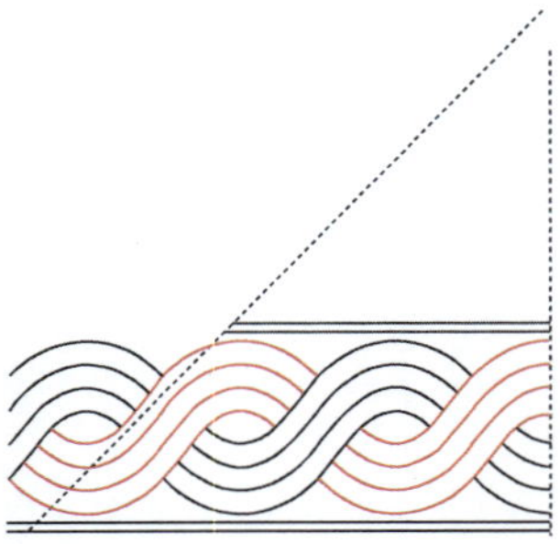

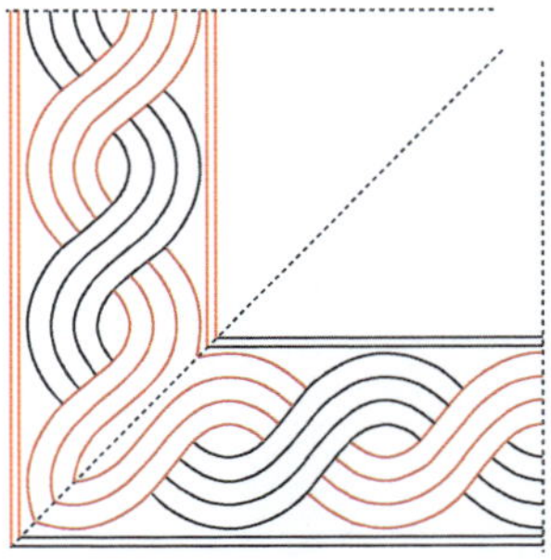

This change in flow at the corner can give a pleasing effect. However, when the quarter design is either mirror-imaged or rotated around the centre of the quilt, the change in flow of the cable becomes more noticeable, especially in the centre of each border.

To create a cable border where the sequence of the under/over twists are consistent, the area where the cables overlap is omitted when tracing the second part of the border.

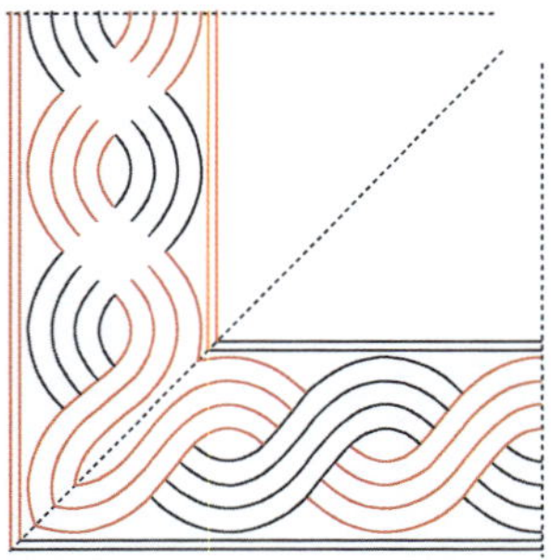

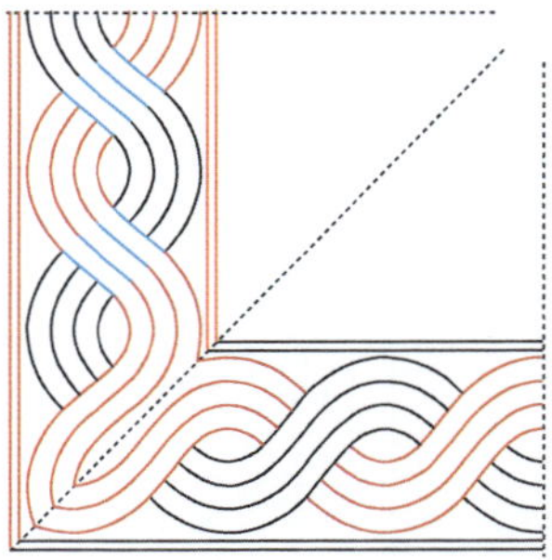

It is then a simple matter of re-joining the lines in the correct direction.

When this quarter section is rotated around the centre, this adjustment now gives a continuous under/over design along each cable border. The sequence is still disrupted at the corners but this could easily remain as a valid design choice.

Similarly, an alternative version can be created by adjusting the corner lines rather than those in the cable. This is achieved by extending the black lines in each corner and erasing the red lines where the two cables cross.

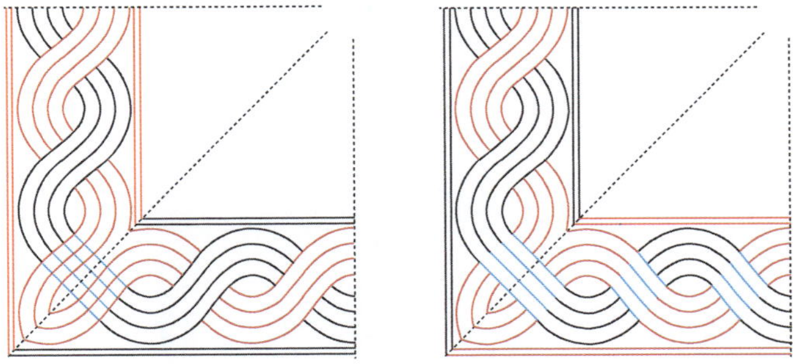

However, for the under/over sequence to remain continuous in the centre of the border, it is also necessary to adjust the cross-over areas on the original cable section.

In the 'classic' version of the cable border, not only should the under/over pattern be continuous around the entire quilt, the cables should also interlock at the corners.

This can be achieved by adjusting the crossover pattern as before.
This time, not only are the crossover patterns reversed on the border on one side of the corner; they are also reversed on that side of the diagonal fold at the corner.

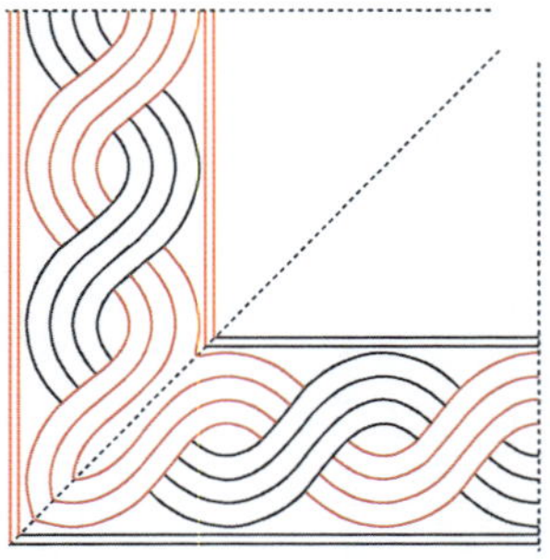

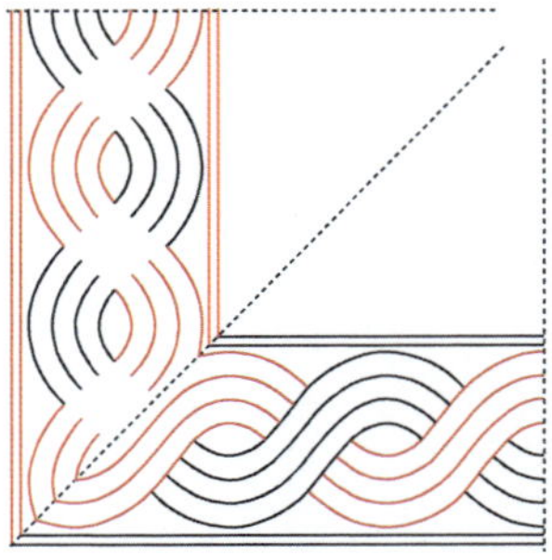

The lines are then extended across the corner to meet the other cable.

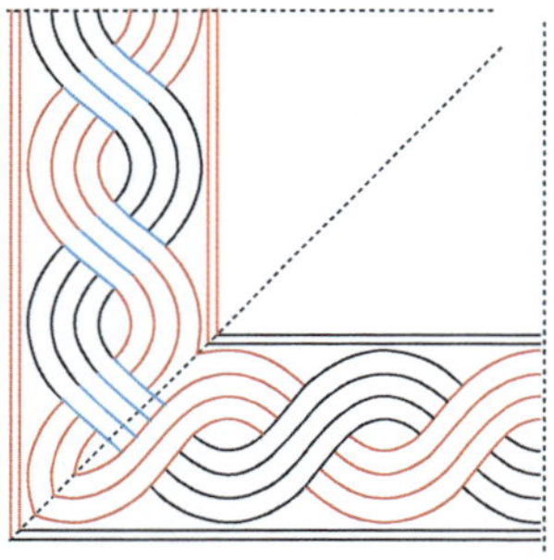

When rotated around the centre of the design, a symmetrical border with a totally continuous under/over sequence will be formed.

A non-traditional (but easy) final alternative is to make the strands of both cables continuous by joining all lines where they cross.

If all the joins are made initially, selected lines can then be erased to form other interesting possibilities.

Not all cable borders are fully symmetrical. One option is to have symmetry around opposing corners. Although the under/over sequence remains broken at the corners, this design gives the illusion of continuous flow.

How the corner turns and which option offer the best solution will very much depend on the length of the border within a design.

If no pleasing solution can be found, it may be better to find a good position in the cable at which to turn the corner and then stretch/shrink the cable to fit the required border length.

Rectangular Quilts

Frequently, old double bed Welsh quilts were not truly square to allow extra length to accommodate covering pillows. Single bed and cot quilts are truly rectangular and therefore pose greater design challenges as they are not totally symmetrical.

The central design of rectangular quilts needs to be in harmony with its overall shape. Therefore, the starting point for this type of quilt is frequently an oblong, oval or an elongated diamond-shaped design.

Seren Bach *Sandie Lush 2005*

Central Motifs for Rectangular Quilts

Oblong central motifs are easier to create than diamond or oval motifs.

The central motif in the quilt shown on the opposite page was created using a variant of the method described on page 64.

Rotating the tip of a leaf motif around a central point in steps of 60 degrees (rather than the original 45) will yield an elongated motif.

This six-fold repeat was created by drawing a vertical guideline onto a piece of paper and then measuring the other 60 degree angles using either a protractor or a quilting ruler.

Each petal of the resultant shape was filled with veins and an outer echo line added.

The design shape can be further stretched by inserting a motif (or part motif) into the spaces between the leaves.

To enlarge the original motif in this way, it is necessary to rotate it by 30 degrees before the addition of any extra pattern.

If the motif is inserted identically around the rotated pattern, the design becomes larger but not particularly elongated.

However, if the portion of the inserted motif visible on the north/south central axis is greater than at the other four points, there is a dramatic elongation of the design.

Adding spirals to the same motif can also extend the design. Again, these are added into the spaces between the leaves. This on its own has little effect other than to enlarge the motif.

However, if the design is rotated back to its original position and additional spirals added to leaf-tips on the north/south central axis, the design will now fit into an elongated diamond shape perfect for a rectangular quilt.

The elongated diamond shape can also be constructed by rotating a square design by 45 degrees and positioning it within an elongated diamond-shaped outline.

The empty spaces can then be filled with smaller motifs.

The square motif can be extended into the new shape by the addition of a leaf motif above and below the centre. Any remaining spaces can then be filled with spiral and echo lines.

A more unusual approach would be to contain some of these designs within a cropped shape rather than within the more traditional rectangular or diamond shapes.

This approach can be particularly useful if the elongated diamond motif is slightly too large to fit the central space.

The diamond can be cropped both horizontally and vertically. For crop B, it was necessary to adjust the position of the leaf motif.

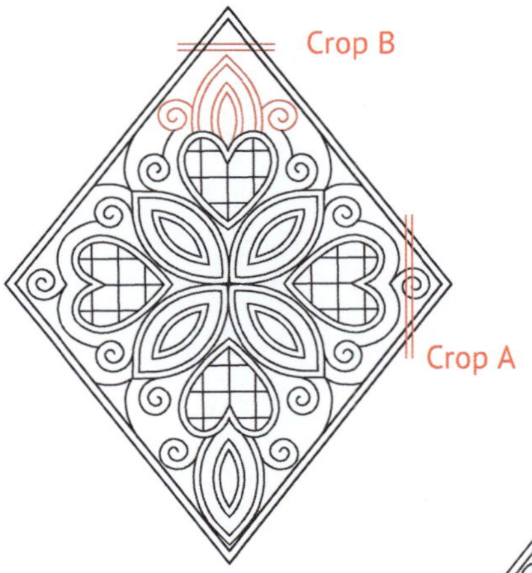

Crop A only

Crop A and B

Oval-shaped central motifs are less common as they are more complicated to construct. As before, they can be made by manipulating a leaf shape.

By changing the angle of the leaf, the design can be adjusted to fit into an oval shape instead of a circle.

Circular shape

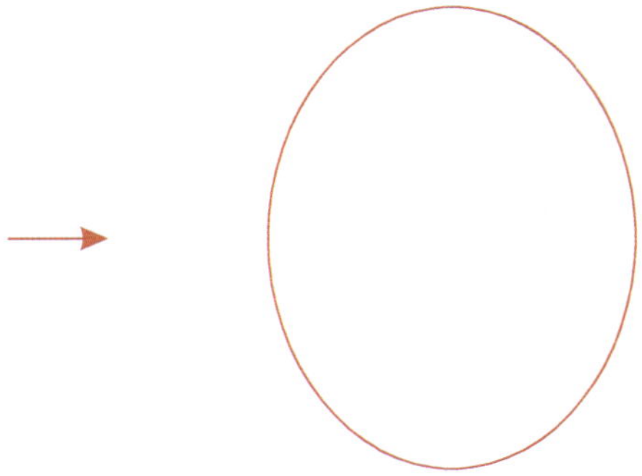

New oval shape

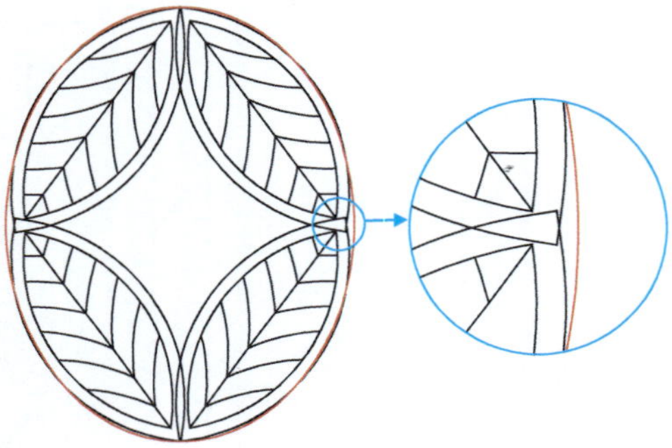

The leaves are angled to fit this new shape. (Echo lines may overlap at this point.)

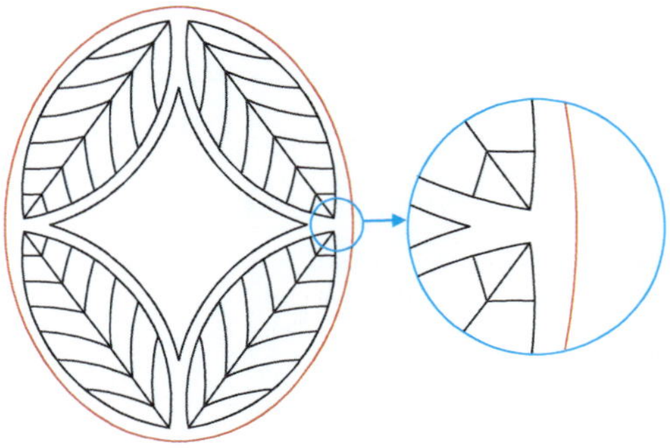

Any overlapping echo lines can then be removed.

This new shape can be further 'tidied up' if required.

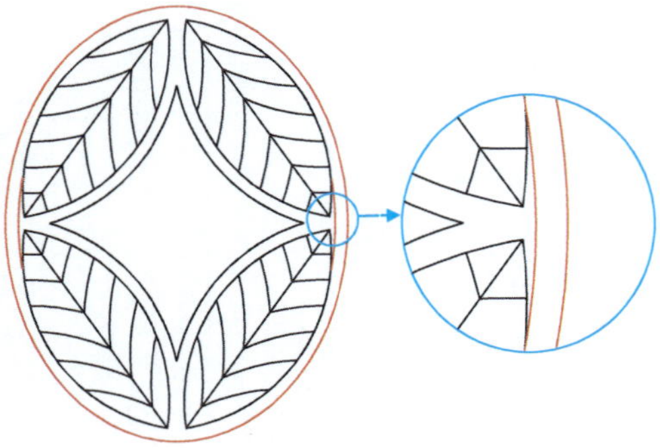

Firstly, an echo line is added to the inside of the new oval shape.

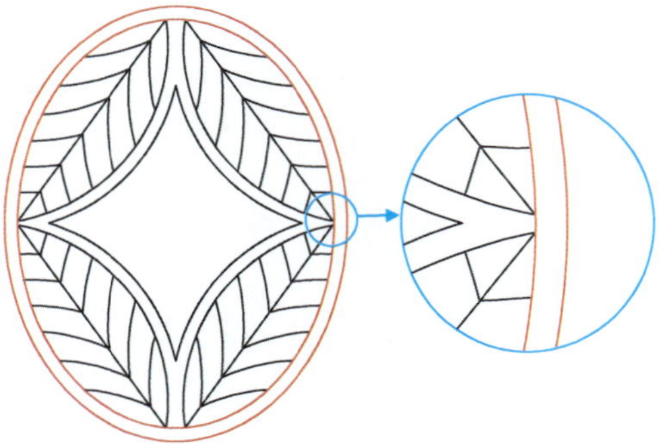

The leaf fill is then adjusted to fit and the outer edges of the leaf removed.

Oval centres can also can be made by manipulating other leaf shapes.

Oval designs can also be extended into elongated and cropped diamond shapes.

When filling the point of the diamond shape it is useful to note that some motifs are more easily cropped than others.

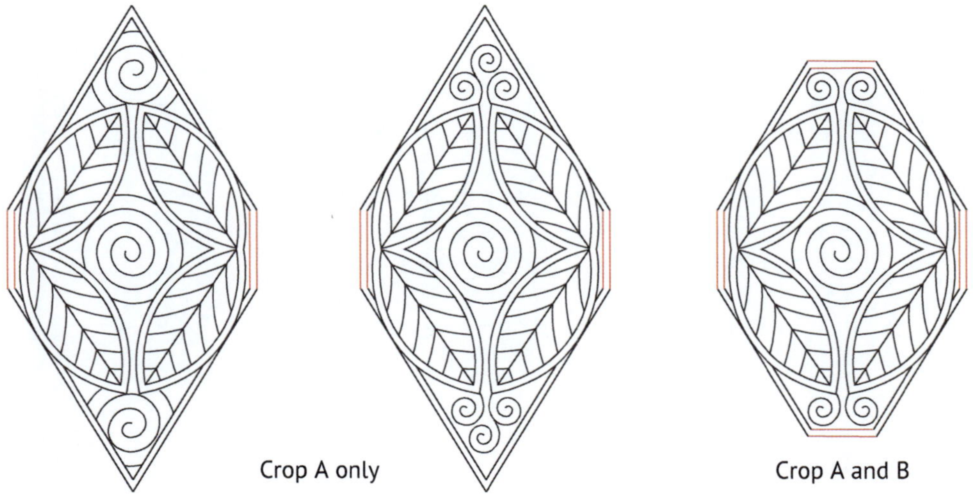

Crop A only

Crop A and B

More complex elongated centres can also be created from asymmetrical motifs.

A six-fold repeat of any motif will yield a shape that is longer than it is wide, although how obvious and what size this difference is will depend on the motif and its orientation.

The positioning of the motifs in the third design can be adjusted into a more obvious oval shape suitable for use in rectangular-shaped quilts.

Firstly, the top and bottom motifs are moved further apart.

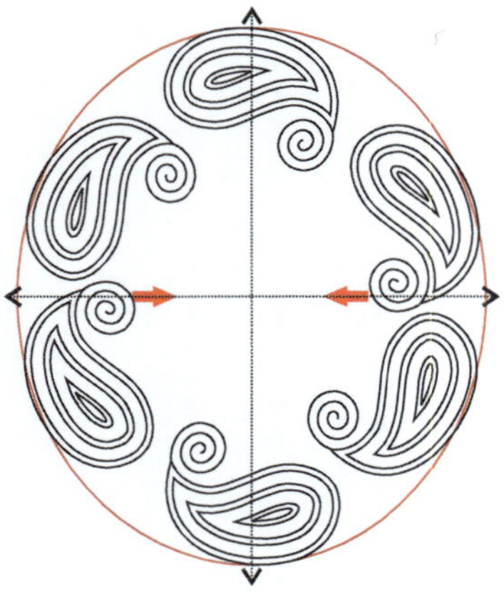

The side pairs of motifs can then be moved inwards to accentuate the oval shape.

Sometimes the original top and bottom motifs may need a slight adjustment to prevent them overlapping.

Although more difficult to draft, is also possible to construct an oval design using the fan shape. The first step is to create radiating lines from the centre of the required oval shape.

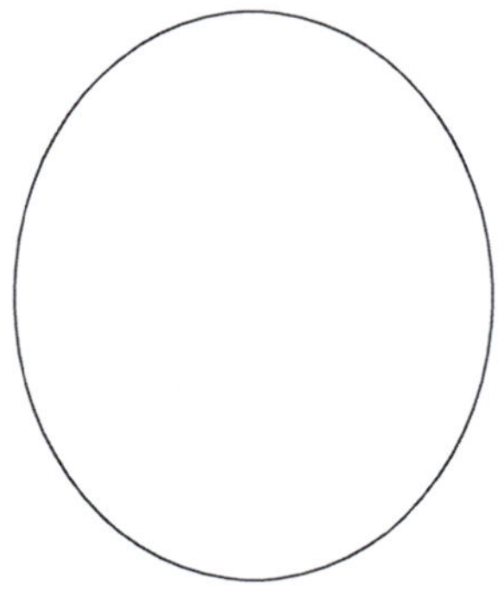

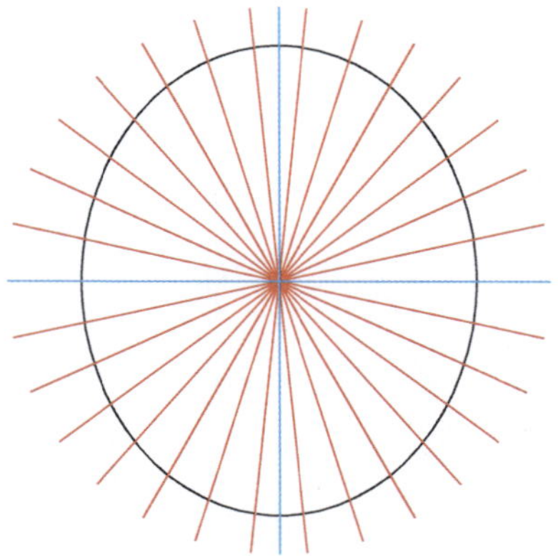

A curved or pointed fan edge can be placed in each small segment. It will be necessary to slightly adjust these edges where they join, but only a quarter of the oval needs to be completed as the rest can be mirror-imaged from this.

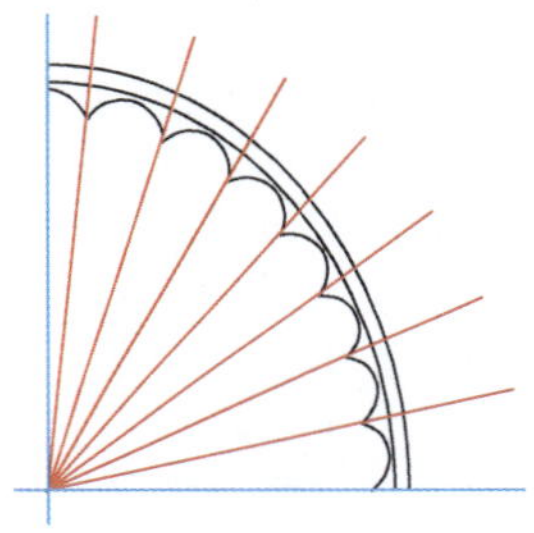

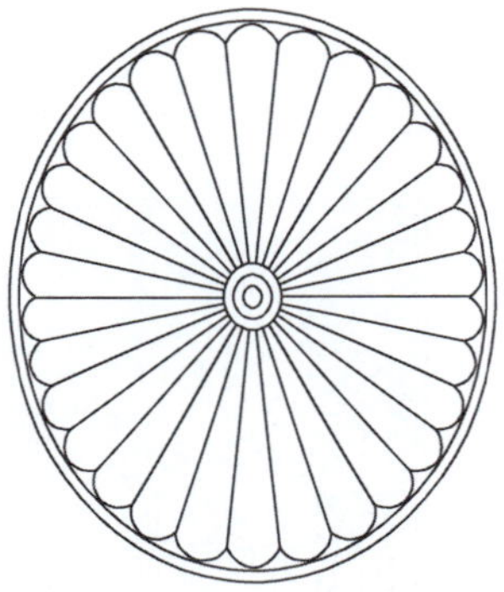

The addition of a small central motif will make stitching easier where multiple lines converge at the centre.

Oval designs may also be extended with the addition of a surrounding border. This is again achieved by positioning each motif either on or between the original guidelines around the centre.

The outer tramlines can then be created by measuring with a quilting ruler using the inner tramlines as guides.

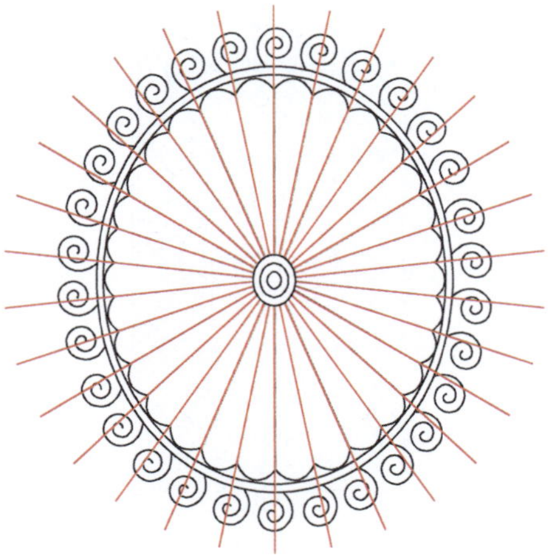

Once the oval, elongated or cropped diamond shape has been created, it needs to be contained within a rectangular shape and the resulting spaces filled.

The filling needs to complement the central motif.

There may not always be the time or inclination to create an elongated central motif from first principles.

Traditionally, the simplest method used to create an elongated central design is to stretch the surrounding 'box' of a square design into a rectangle. This example uses the design from page 70.

Depending on how far the rectangular shape is stretched, the area remaining to be filled with background quilting can become quite large and noticeably asymmetrical.

This can be addressed by the addition of another pattern. Not only will this reduce the disparity in the amount of background quilting around the central motif, it will also add more visual interest. Simply filling the top and bottom spaces with a spiral or clamshell border will give a greater illusion of symmetry (A), but with practice more ornate designs can be created (B).

A

B

Adding Borders to Rectangular Quilts

Once the central rectangle has been created, it is a simple matter to add borders to create a cot or single quilt.

The size and number of borders added will determine the finished size of the quilt.

A rectangular (and therefore asymmetrical) shape allows a number of options for how the borders can be placed around the centre. Corner boxes make the process easier, but there is no rule that says they must be used for every border, or even used at all. In fact, when corner boxes are not used for every border, further design options are created by varying the sequence in which borders are added.

Decisions concerning the way in which borders are added may be influenced by personal preference but are usually governed by how the chosen patterns best fit the space.

To illustrate this point, the final medallion design from page 117 was extended with the addition of a surrounding Welsh square border. This generates several design possibilities.

The usual practice is to create corner boxes as shown in options 1 and 2.

1

2

This particular border has the potential to dispense with the corner box.
If the box is not used and the border does not form a perfect continuous fit, a decision has to be taken as to whether the longer borders travel down the length of the quilt...

3

4

...or whether they travel across the width of the quilt.

There is a choice to be made concerning the central placement of the borders.

For each pair of examples shown, the odd numbered diagrams have the horizontal borders centred on the middle of the diamond and the vertical borders centred on the point where two diamond shapes meet. For the even numbered diagrams, the reverse applies.

All six illustrated options have excellent design potential.

To reach a decision as to which option to use, various design aspects need to be considered.

The two most important aspects are the motifs used in the border and the shapes in which those motifs are contained. Welsh squares is a very versatile border and the basic shapes can be filled in a seemingly infinite number of ways. Therefore, looking at the positioning of the empty containing shapes can be useful at this stage because subsequent fillings and motifs can easily be altered or replaced.

The relative placement of the border 'squares' is an important consideration.

It can be seen in options 3, 4 and 5 that, with a little time and manipulation, the design could be made to turn the corner (adjustment of the side border motifs could lead to the tramlines being removed entirely).

Options 3 and 5 offer a fairly continuous motif placement. Option 3 can be considered the more aesthetically pleasing of the two as its longer borders run the length of the quilt, thus accentuating the rectangular nature of the design.

Option 4 has a less traditional look. In this case border placement yields an unusual corner, but this could be resolved if alternate squares were filled differently and replicated around the quilt.

3

4

5

Placement of the inner triangles could be regarded as equally important.

These may only comprise a small part of the border pattern, but the designs they contain sit closest to the motifs making up the centre medallion.

In options 2, 4, and 6 the inner triangles totally enclose the centre medallion and form a continuous frame around it.

Some of the inner triangles also enhance and add to the shape formed by the spirals in the centre.

2

4

6

The final choice may be determined by technical or even artistic considerations. It is important to remember that personal preference plays a very important part in the creative process.

Having carefully considered all the options, it was decided that placement of the inner triangles to form a secondary design was the most pleasing. This led to the rejection of options 1, 3 and 5.

Option 4 was also rejected because of the length of time it would take to adjust the vertical patterns to provide a better match at the corners.

It was felt option 6 was slightly quirky and had a good 'Welsh' feel to it. It also avoided having to choose a motif for a corner box (as in option 2).

A Welsh square border from page 43 was chosen to fill the shapes.

To ensure continuity with the motifs already used in the central medallion, the leaf fillings were adapted to match and a grid pattern substituted for the diagonal lines.

The design was then finished with an outer border of spirals.

How the spirals were arranged to fit around the design is explained on page 35.

The design can be increased in size by the addition of further borders.

Elongation can be achieved by using a motif that can be orientated differently to form narrow or wide borders.

The leaf motif used in the centre of the quilt is perfect in this case because it lends continuity to the design. How to position the motif is described on page 76.

Since this motif is symmetrical in shape, its size can easily be adjusted to fit around the whole design.

The outer row of small spirals again gives a sense of completion to the finished design and provides continuity with the inner spiral border.

Another way to elongate a design is to choose a motif that can be used in either single or double format, so creating borders of differing widths. Using this approach can produce differences in border size on a larger scale.

Using the grid system, the motifs can be accurately placed to form a continuous border.

In this example, the top and bottom (double) borders were positioned first. The long (single) border was then divided into equal boxes. This determined the position and angle at which the leaf was placed to form a continuous chain.

Once again the design was then finished with a row of spirals.

The central heart motif can also be manipulated to form borders using the grid system in a similar fashion to the leaf.

How the heart is filled raises some interesting design issues.

To form the double heart outer border, opposite, the motif was rotated by 45 degrees.

This noticeably changed the orientation of the grid filling, as shown below.

To maintain continuity of design, it then became necessary to change the orientation of the grid filling in the central heart.

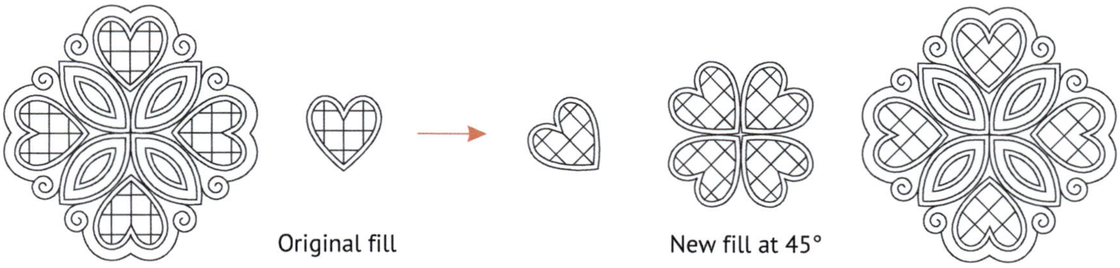

However, with both the Welsh square and heart motifs both now having grid fillings in the same orientation, the design lacked contrast. To remedy this, the Welsh square fill was changed to simple straight lines.

It was also necessary to flip the entire Welsh square border to separate the small heart motifs contained in the triangles from the larger heart motifs in the outer border.

These small changes give the quilt a totally different look.

Although it can be easier to start with an elongated central design, it is not always necessary. As already demonstrated, using asymmetric borders makes it reasonably straightforward to extend a design into a rectangular shaped quilt. This technique can also be applied to either square or circular central motifs.
Firstly, a circular design similar to those shown on page 62 was created.

A leaf motif was used to create both double and single borders as in the design on page 126. However, a more complex leaf filling was devised to confer harmony with the central design.

Positioning the double border above and below the centrepiece converted the design into a rectangular shape. For added interest, the centre pair of leaves were flipped horizontally to form a circular design and a rose placed in the central space.
The single side borders could then be placed.

To help fill the remaining central space, a small cable border enclosed by tramlines was added between the leaf border and the centrepiece. The remaining spaces were filled with echo or diagonal lines.

The design was then finished with an outer border of the same small cable.

This quilt is shown opposite and its reverse on page 145.

Croeso *Sandie Lush 2017*

Using more than one double border will extend a design to an even greater degree.

In this example the addition of a double spiral border enlarges and elongates a cot-sized design into one suitable for a child's bed.

Similarly, to extend this design to a single bed-sized quilt, further border(s) would need to be added.

An alternative strategy for enlarging this design would be to increase the scale by 50%. This would convert the tramline widths from a 1/4" to 3/8" and the patterns would become correspondingly larger.

Another simple way to convert a square or circular design into a rectangular one is by the addition of an extra border on two opposing sides of the quilt.

One way to achieve this is to add the extra border at the outset.

With this approach, the rectangular shape is already set, and it is a simple matter to add further borders of equal width to bring the design to the required size.

In this design, the spacing of both tramlines and background fillings was 3/8", i.e. to a scale appropriate for a single bed. Reducing the scale by 33% would yield a cot-sized quilt.

It is also relatively simple to extend this design into a square quilt to fit a double bed.

Positioning the inner rose border on all four sides of the central motif (rather than just two) would create a square design.

It would then be necessary to fill the newly created corner boxes. However, this is the only new design element introduced, as the outer long borders still fit on all four sides of the design.

The previous example extended the design at the outset, but with some designs leaving this until a later stage can be advantageous.

This second approach can be especially useful when using patterns such as the church window border, which need to be of a particular size in order to turn the corner effectively.

The centrepiece of the previous quilt was adapted slightly for this second example.

This time, the Welsh trail border was used for the borders surrounding the central motif. The corner boxes were filled with the diamond element of this motif and straight lines aligned with the cable lines were added to fill the remaining space to provide an illusion of continuous flow.

Next, the church window pattern was created and positioned around the quilt centre.

How (and where) the pattern turned the corner in a pleasing fashion determined the outer edges of the quilt.

The remaining unfilled area around the centre was now defined by the size and position of the outer border.

Initially the narrow side areas were filled with spirals.

Additional spirals were positioned across the horizontal inner edges of the church window border. The corner spirals were adjusted to form a continuous border.

The remaining area was divided into triangles which were filled with the central rose motif and a combination of curved filling (to echo the curves in the inner border) and diagonal lines (to mirror the straight line fill in the church windows).

This quilt could be finished at this point with a scalloped edge formed by the church window outline.

Alternatively, tramlines could be added to give a straight edge and the quilt finished with an outer spiral border.

Finally, the resultant spaces in the church window border should be filled with echo lines.

Often, square designs can easily be converted into rectangular quilts by removing borders on two opposing sides.

The above quilt (a slight variation on the design on page 86) may be adapted in two different ways. These are shown on the opposite page.

Version A was formed by removing the side leaf borders and their corner boxes.

Version B was formed by removing the side Welsh square borders and their corner boxes.

Obviously, a change in width will affect the size of the outer border, and the placement of motifs may need some adjustment.
For version A, it was necessary to increase the spacing of the spirals in the horizontal borders.

Other borders may also need minor adjustment.
For version B, it was necessary to also increase the spacing of the leaf motifs in the horizontal borders.

Different effects are achieved according to which borders are removed. Although both single quilts opposite are derived from the same original square design, the version which retains the fans (A) is slightly smaller than the one from which they have been removed (B).

A

B

Scale

Given the huge range of motifs and size options available, keeping the choice of patterns used in a Welsh quilt design to an appropriate scale can be quite difficult.

Borders made from small motifs will have more impact in a cot quilt than if used in a large bed quilt design where they may get 'lost'. Where small borders are found in large quilts, they are often acting as tramlines to divide patterns, or are positioned on the outer edges of the quilt design.

The reverse would also be true as large motifs can easily overwhelm a smaller design. Smaller old Welsh quilts with large designs do exist, but it often transpires they were originally bigger quilts that have been cut down to size.

The centre of this design is more suited to a large quilt.

The border is scaled for a cot-sized design, making the centre disproportionately large for the scale of the surrounding border.

Small scale motifs combined to create a centre pattern are more suitable.

In this design, the scale in the centre is in keeping with that in the surrounding border.

Some motifs can be used in quilts of any size. For example, a leaf shape can typically range from 1" to 24" in size.

How that leaf shape is filled is equally as important as the shape itself. A small leaf used to create a chain border will not need any filling or outlining. A 2" leaf will require only a centre spine and possibly a single pair of veins. An increase in size will require an increase in the number of veins added.

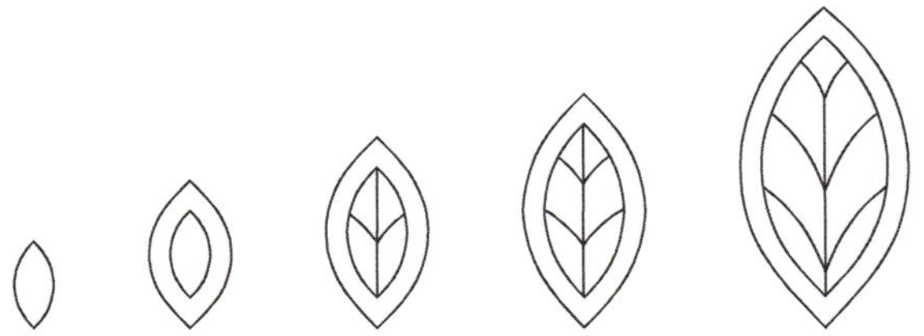

On a larger scale it is the spacing of both the filling lines and the outlines which determine whether the scale is suited to a small or large quilt.

At full scale, leaf A has a 1/4" outline suitable for a large motif in a small quilt...

...leaf B has a 3/8" outline suitable for a small motif in a large quilt...

...leaf C is only suitable for a large quilt.

A

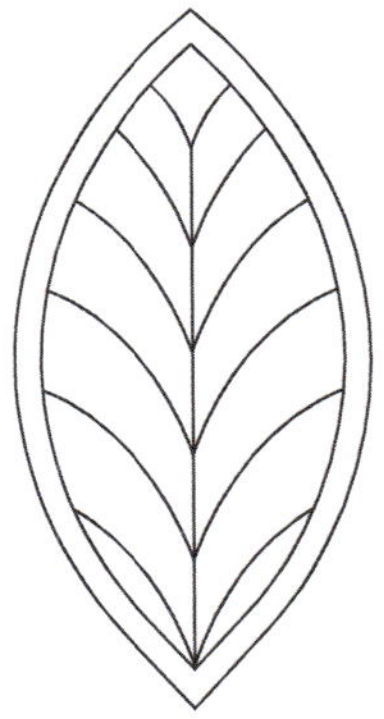

B

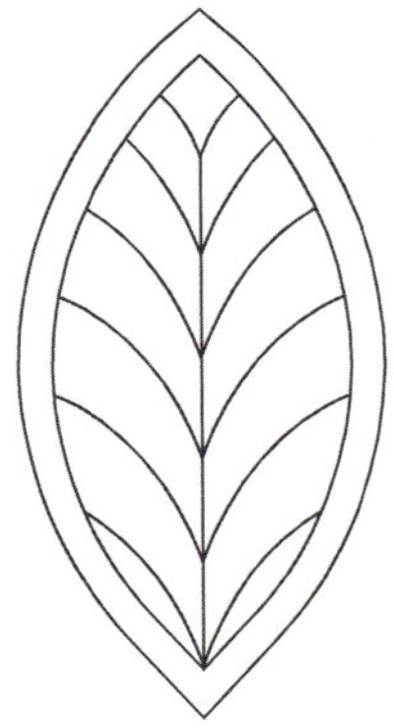

C

Patterns may easily be enlarged or reduced using a photocopier or scanner, but the spacing of the fillings inside as well as the echo lines will invariably need adjusting.

It is not just the width of the defining tramlines that needs adjustment according to the size of the finished design. The scale of background quilting around the motifs will also need to be adjusted.

Tramlines used for cot and small quilt designs are usually either a 1/4" or 3/8" apart. Any background or echo quilting needs to be spaced differently for the motifs to retain definition. This is achieved by making those lines further apart. Therefore, 1/4" tramlines would have echo/filling lines no less than 3/8" apart, and 3/8" tramlines would have echo/filling lines no less than a 1/2" apart.

Bed quilt designs are normally larger, so either 3/8" or 1/2" tramlines are more appropriate. Background or echo filling would need to be correspondingly larger and 5/8", 3/4" or even 1" spacing would be suitable.

Consideration also needs to be given to how the pattern will 'translate' when the design is actually quilted.

Very dense lines look marvellous on paper but may prove disappointing on a finished quilt. Quilting stitches compress the fabric and wadding together, forcing them into the background and, as a result, it is the surrounding unstitched spaces that tend to stand out. Looking at a quilting design can be regarded as viewing a black and white negative of how the design will actually appear in the finished quilt.

A four-leaf motif with suitably spaced surrounding echo lines can be used to illustrate this point.

The motif can be filled with 'veins' (A) or echoes (B).

A

Although dramatic on paper, if the leaf filling is spaced too closely together the motif is simply pushed into the background and recedes from view when stitched.

This is even more apparent if the leaf is filled with echoes.

B

When alternate filling lines are removed, the 'veins' become more obvious.

The same applies to the surrounding background quilting.

The above examples only utilised alternate echo lines to ensure the leaf tramlines retained their impact.

Multiple echo lines may look impressive on paper but, as shown below, if stitched the same distance apart as the tramlines surrounding the leaf, the motif loses definition. In these examples the leaf filling 'floats' on a sea of dense quilting.

It is usual for the borders and/or motifs to increase in size towards the outer edges of the quilt. However, smaller borders that have another border on either side could be regarded as several small borders or one large one.
There are no hard and fast rules, but where small borders are used in place of tramlines the size of these ideally remain constant throughout the quilt design.

Increasing the size of pattern out from the centre takes the eye towards the edge of the quilt. However, a small outer confining border (such as a spiral border) can be added to give the design a sense of completion.

As well as considering scale, it is also important to maintain some kind of continuity within the design. With so many ways to fill motifs and spaces, it can be tempting to use too wide a variety resulting in the overall design becoming lost in the detail.

Basically, good quilt design is about achieving a balance of scale and a harmony of pattern.

Always remember that the closer together the lines of quilting stitches are, the more impressive they look on paper but the less impact they have on the finished quilt. Without the uncompressed spaces between lines of stitching, the patterns become lost in the background. The reverse is also true, and a large unquilted area of background will visually dwarf the areas of more densely stitched pattern it surrounds.

Importantly, it is the overall balance and spacing of the stitching lines that give Welsh quilts their wonderful sculptural appearance.

Within the Welsh style there is great flexibility and enormous potential for variation in design. This makes designing Welsh quilts both very exciting yet somewhat daunting to tackle.

Stitching from the ‘plain’ side makes life easier when marking and stitching a quilt and creates excitement and a very Welsh look should the reverse be simple strips of fabric or some form of patchwork. It was usual for the patchwork side of a quilt to be the ‘everyday’ side, leaving the plain side for special occasions such as a visit from the doctor or the minister!

When creating your own Welsh quilt, be guided by personal preference and remember that some of the most charming old Welsh quilts are the ones that are not quite ‘perfect’. Many designs were hand drawn directly onto fabric and minor (and even major) adjustments to the design were frequently necessary. We would not consciously design that way now, but that extra spiral or the squashed leaf in the design only adds to the quirky charms of those treasured antique quilts.

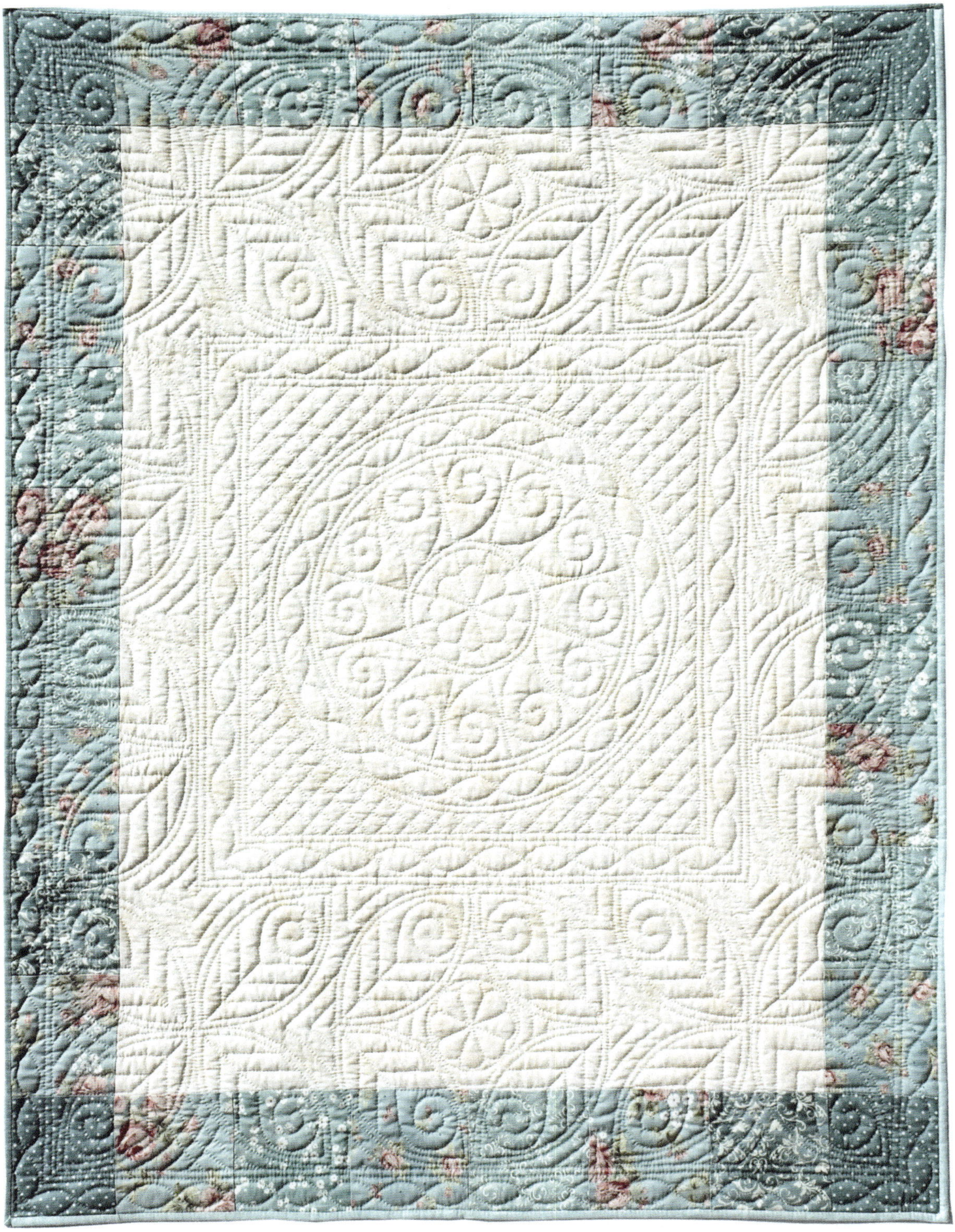

Croeso (reverse) *Sandie Lush 2017*

Materials and methods

Fabrics

The most prized of old Welsh quilts are those made of woollen flannel. At least one side of these quilts were mostly big bold patchworks, but both sides would have featured the flannel fabric. Other quilts were made of linen, cotton (both printed and plain), cotton sateen and even silk. Expensive items such as Paisley shawls were utilised whereas other quilts used anything that came to hand, including tailor's samples and other scraps. More modern quilts used the new fabrics such as rayon and polyester type fabrics as well as the old favourites.

Larger quilts need fabric to be joined to create a single piece. It is usual to avoid a central seam by joining three panels so that the seams lay either side of the centre.

Threads

In earlier times there was not the variety of thread available today and old quilts were stitched in thick brown, black or cream thread.

Nowadays the choice of thread can be overwhelming. A 40wt machine quilting thread works well for hand quilting. For those who have a larger quilting stitch, a 30wt top stitching thread or even thicker thread (such as perlé 12) would show the stitches to better effect. Choosing a colour slightly darker than the fabric used will give added dimension to the finished quilt by highlighting the pattern and accentuating the fact that the stitches lie in the shadow of the surrounding unquilted areas.

Filling

The Welsh are sheep farmers and the filling in their quilts is wool. This may have been finely hand carded neck hair (which was often enclosed in two layers of cheesecloth to prevent fibre migration), wool gathered from the hedgerows (sometimes washed before use but frequently not) or even especially woven blankets.

Wool wadding (batting) is still available and is lovely to hand quilt. However, should this not be affordable, a good quality 2oz polyester wadding will have the same loft and give the sculptured effect vital to the Welsh style.

Frames and Marking

Finally, the old quilts were hand stitched in large wooden frames. The design was often marked out freehand or by using templates in chalk as the work progressed.

These days a 14" beech quilting hoop is far more practical. As chalk will rub off when using a hoop, it is easier to trace the design onto the fabric before layering the quilt ready for stitching. A simple artist's watercolour pencil is ideal for this as it will wash out later (although it is always a good idea to test this before starting the project). Should this not prove effective there are many other marking products on the market.

It is important when working in any type of frame not to have the work stretched too tightly as this will make returning the needle to the top surface very difficult.

The Hand Quilting Stitch

It is far more important to master even quilting stitches than to attempt tiny ones. Stitches will naturally become smaller with practice, but stitch regularity is something every quilter has to work at.

Size of stitch will not only depend on the stitcher but also on the fabrics used. Old Welsh flannel quilts were incredibly thick and often only two stitches to the inch could be achieved. The weave of a fabric can also affect stitch size - more open weaves being easier to pass a needle through than tightly woven ones. Basically each quilt will be different.

When working in an old-fashioned frame, quilting would commence at one edge and work across the quilt. When working in a hoop it is usual to start stitching from the centre of the quilt and work outwards. The outer parts of the quilt can be finished by tacking a towel to the quilt edges, thus extending the working area of the hoop beyond the edge of the work.

1

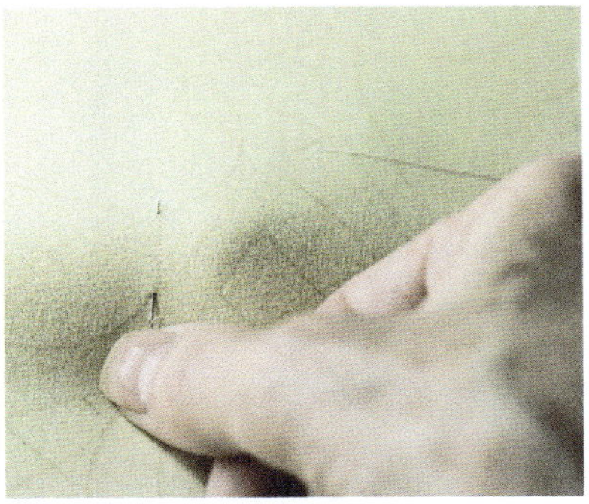

Start by making a knot in the end of about 18" of thread.
Insert the needle into the wadding (but not the backing fabric) and under the stitching line about 1/2" (1.25 cm) in from its starting point. Slide the needle through the wadding until the point of the needle comes up at this starting position. (When burying the knot, the needle initially travels in the opposite direction to the intended direction of stitching.)

2

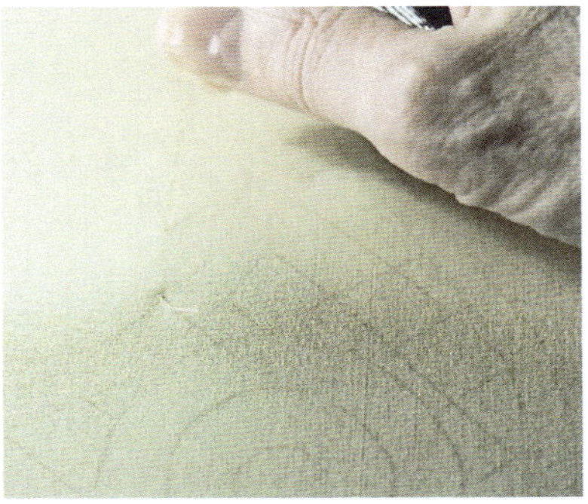

Pull the thread through so that the knot 'pops' between the fibres of the fabric and into the wadding. If the knot does not appear to want to go through, do not force the issue but start again: the needle may have split a fibre in the fabric, and forcing the knot through will make a hole.

3

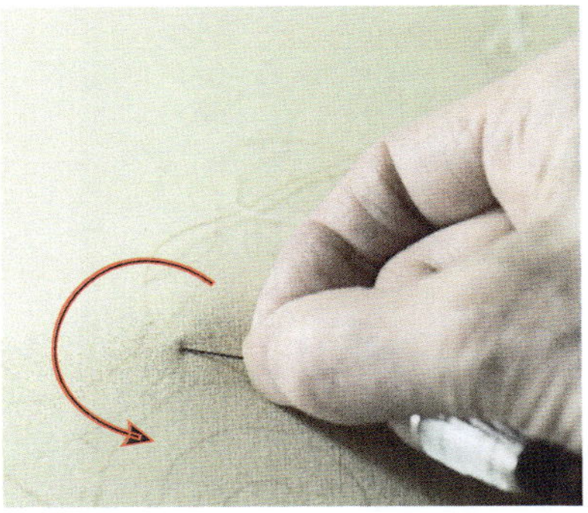

Any small tail of thread can be dealt with by sliding the needle under it and rotating the needle horizontally until the thread disappears.

4

Start stitching in the normal direction so that the thread will not only be anchored by the knot but also by the stitches formed over it.

Mastering the quilting stitch requires practice!

The most usual (and painless) way to quilt is by using two thimbles, but other forms of finger protection are available.

Sheer fabrics have been used to show the action of both thimbles during the quilting process.

1

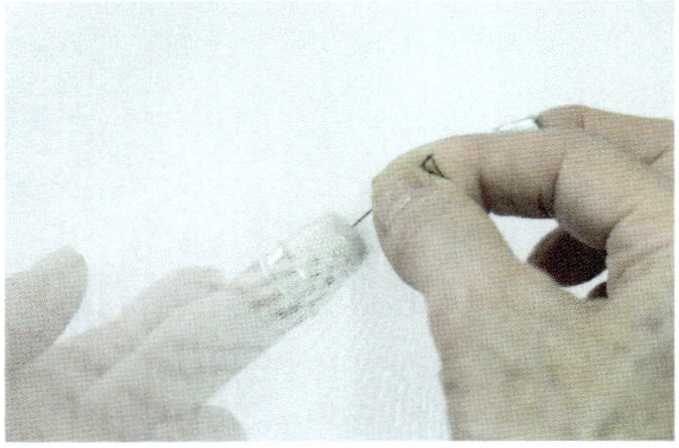

Put the needle into the fabric and onto the top of the underneath thimble at an almost perpendicular angle.

2

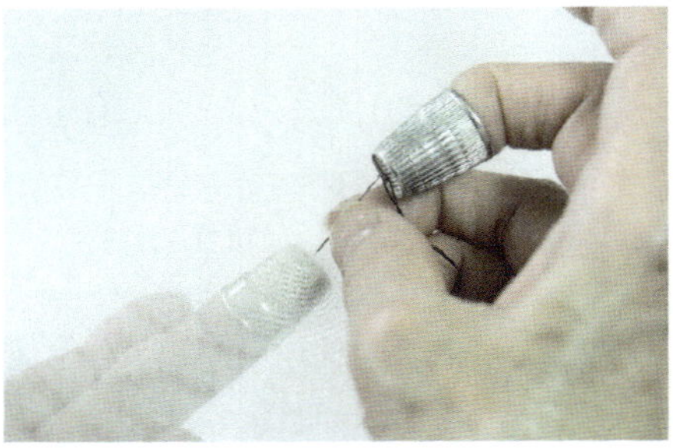

Bring the thimble on the top hand into position so that the needle is balanced between the upper and lower thimbles.

3

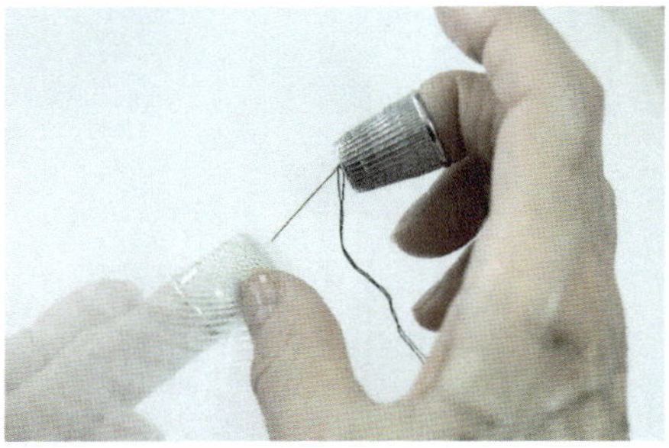

Bring the thumb of the sewing hand forward and rest it on the thimble finger of the underneath hand. This will help bring the needle back up to the surface without creating tension in the wrist of the sewing hand.

4

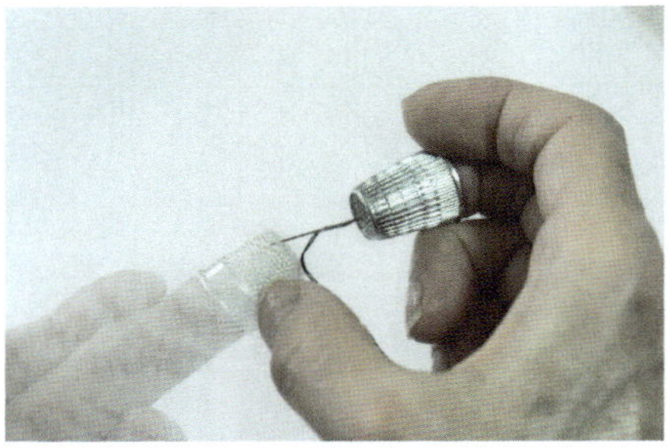

Angle the needle back down towards the fabric and push the underneath thimble so that it is hard up against the tip of the needle.
The gap between the stitches is determined by when the underneath thimble is pushed.

5

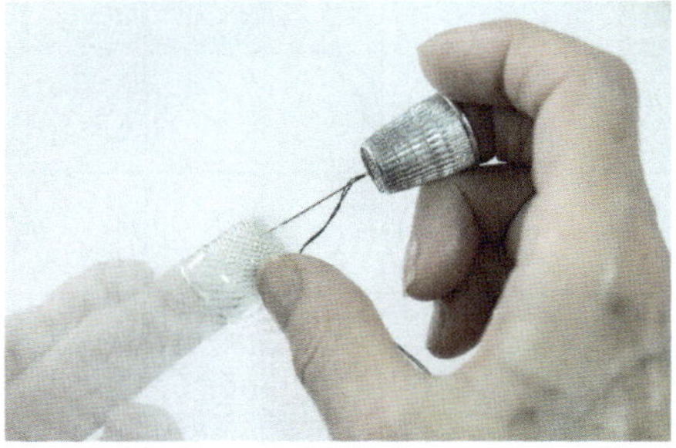

Now push the needle towards the underneath thimble. It should skip off the edge of it and reappear at the surface.
The size of the subsequent stitch is directly determined by how hard the needle is pushed.

6

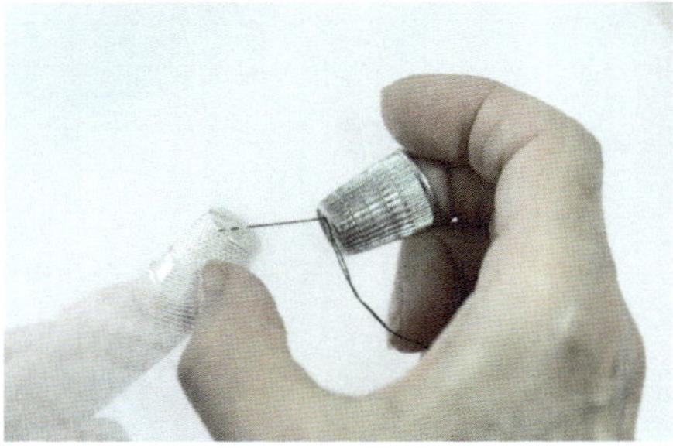

Repeat steps 4 and 5 to create extra stitches before pulling the needle through. With practice, this technique can be used to load the needle with multiple stitches. This number is often governed by the quilting pattern, as fewer stitches can be loaded on curved designs. Fabric thickness may also limit the number of stitches that can be achieved.

It is best to start and finish threads at 'junctions' in the quilting design. When a thread is finished and another started, stitches may skew slightly and not lie evenly. Consequently, starting and finishing in the middle of a smooth curve may spoil its overall appearance.

Generally it is better to waste a small amount of thread and start a new length where the stitching changes direction than interrupt the flow of the design.

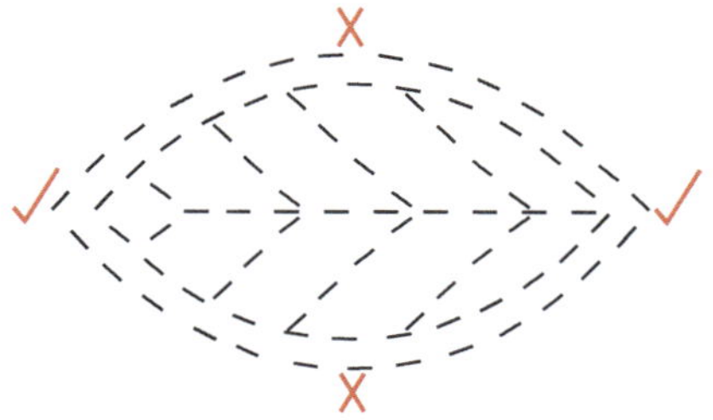

1

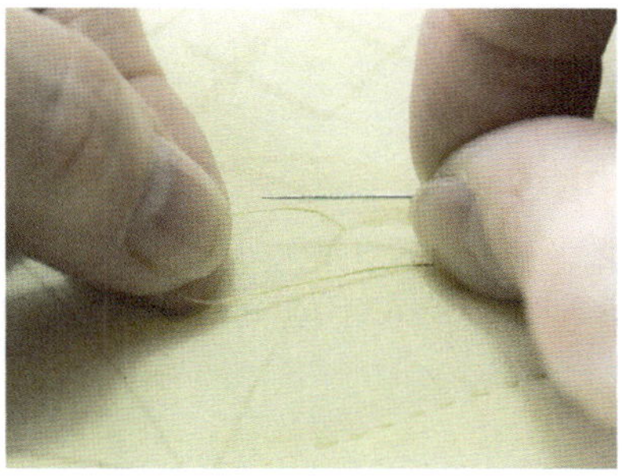

When reaching the end of a thread, leave enough space for one last stitch. Hold the thread coming out of the fabric with the non-sewing hand and bring the needle around, away from the body, to form a loop.

2

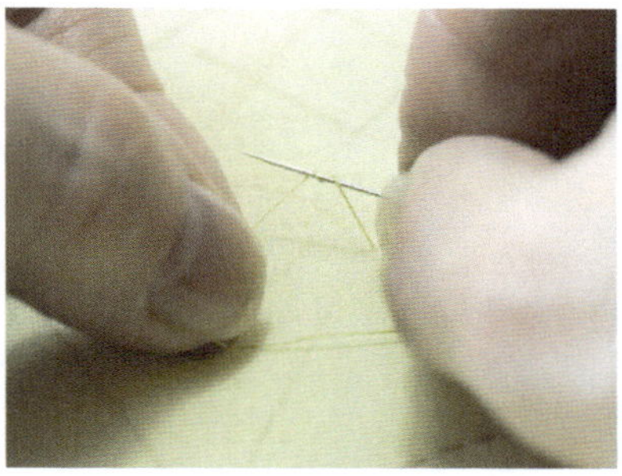

Wrap the thread two or three times around the needle.

3

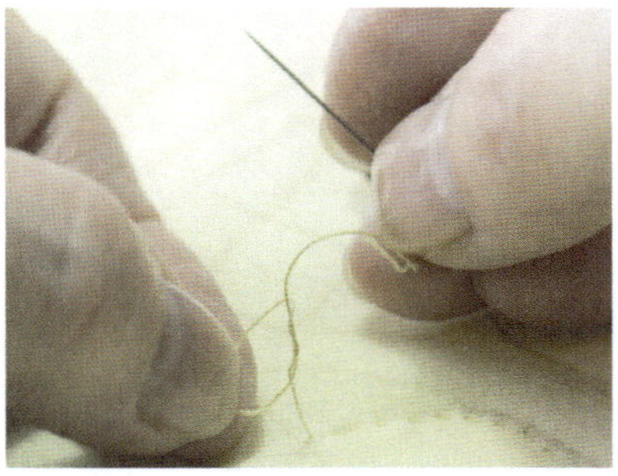

Pull the needle through to form a loose French knot. Be careful not to pull this too tight at this stage.

4

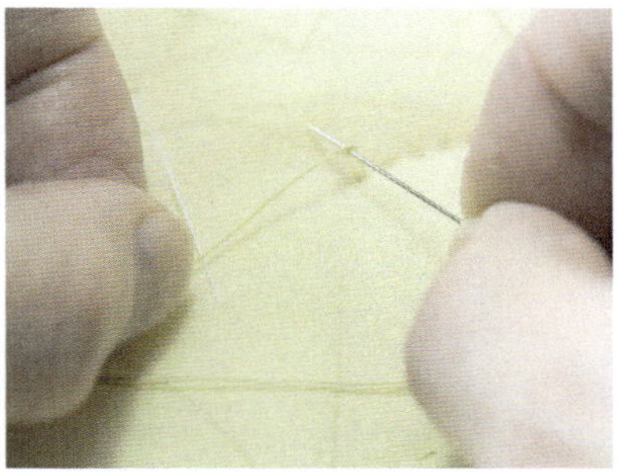

Using the point of the needle, gently tease the knot down towards the quilting until there is only enough thread between the fabric and the knot for one last stitch.

5

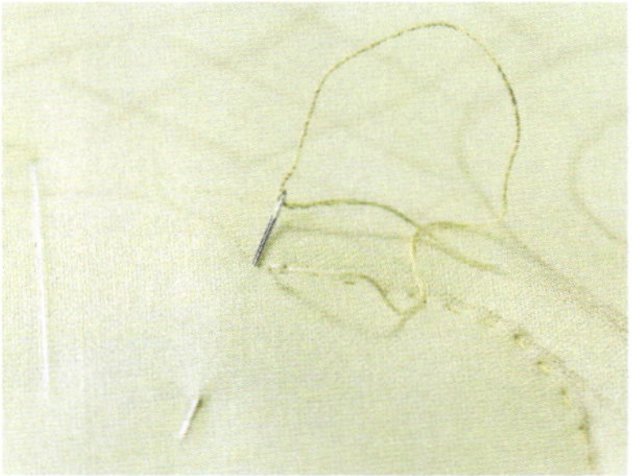

Remove the needle from the knot and insert it into the wadding (but not the backing fabric) to form the last stitch. Ideally, the needle should also travel underneath a pattern line yet to be stitched as this will further anchor the thread.
The needle can be pulled through to the surface to 'pop' the knot and the remaining thread carefully snipped away.

Finishing the Quilt

Although nowadays quilts are usually finished with a binding, the traditional way to complete a Welsh quilt is to fold the outer edges in towards each other.

1

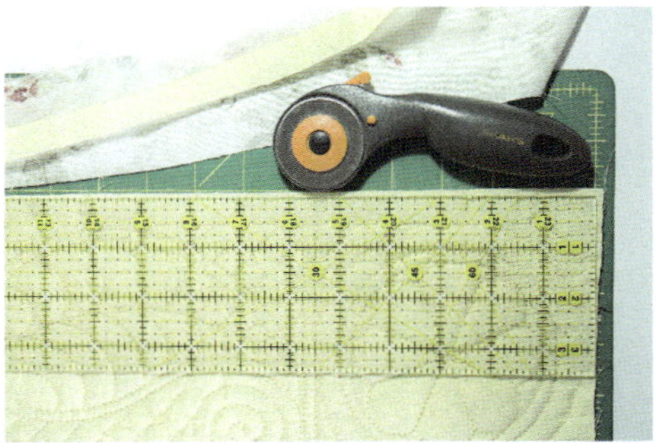

Out from the final stitching line, the very outer edge of the quilt is trimmed through all layers at a distance twice the width of the tramlines used within the design: i.e. for 1/4" tramlines trim the quilt a 1/2" out from the stitching line, for 3/8" tramlines trim 3/4" out, etc.

2

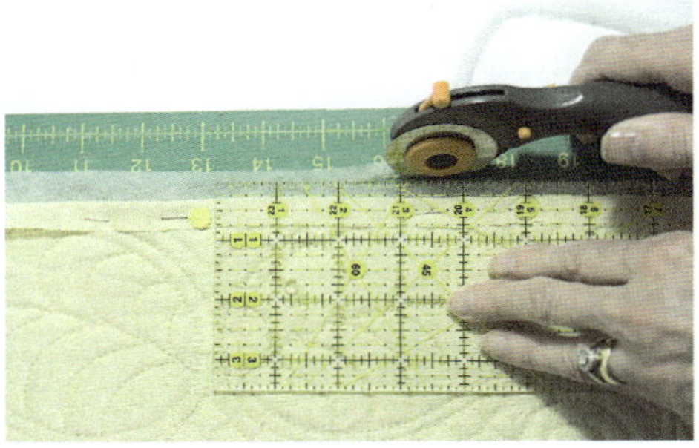

Carefully fold back the top and backing fabrics and trim the wadding by one width of the tramlines used within the design.

3

The wadding should now be one tramline width larger than the outer stitching line but one tramline width smaller than the front and backing fabrics.
Fold the top fabric over and behind the edge of the wadding and secure with pins.

4

Turn the backing fabric in on itself by the same amount and pin in place.

5

As close to the outer edge as possible, secure all layers with a running stitch.
On larger quilts, a second line of stitching can be added between this outer row of stitches and those which outline the pattern.

Dawns Ffan *Sandie Lush 2017*

Appendix

The Motifs

Most of the designs in this book have been drawn to a 1/10th scale. Larger designs may have been reduced further to 1/15th scale or more. However, a few individual motif illustrations have been enlarged to show detail and some may not be in scale with the quilt design diagrams.

This appendix contains basic motif shapes in multiple sizes. There are a few filled examples to generate ideas and provide a starting point from which these shapes can be filled with a choice of patterns both old and new.

The motifs can be made to any size, but the scale of any defining tramlines or fillings will consequently need adjustment.

Heart templates

Leaf/flat iron templates

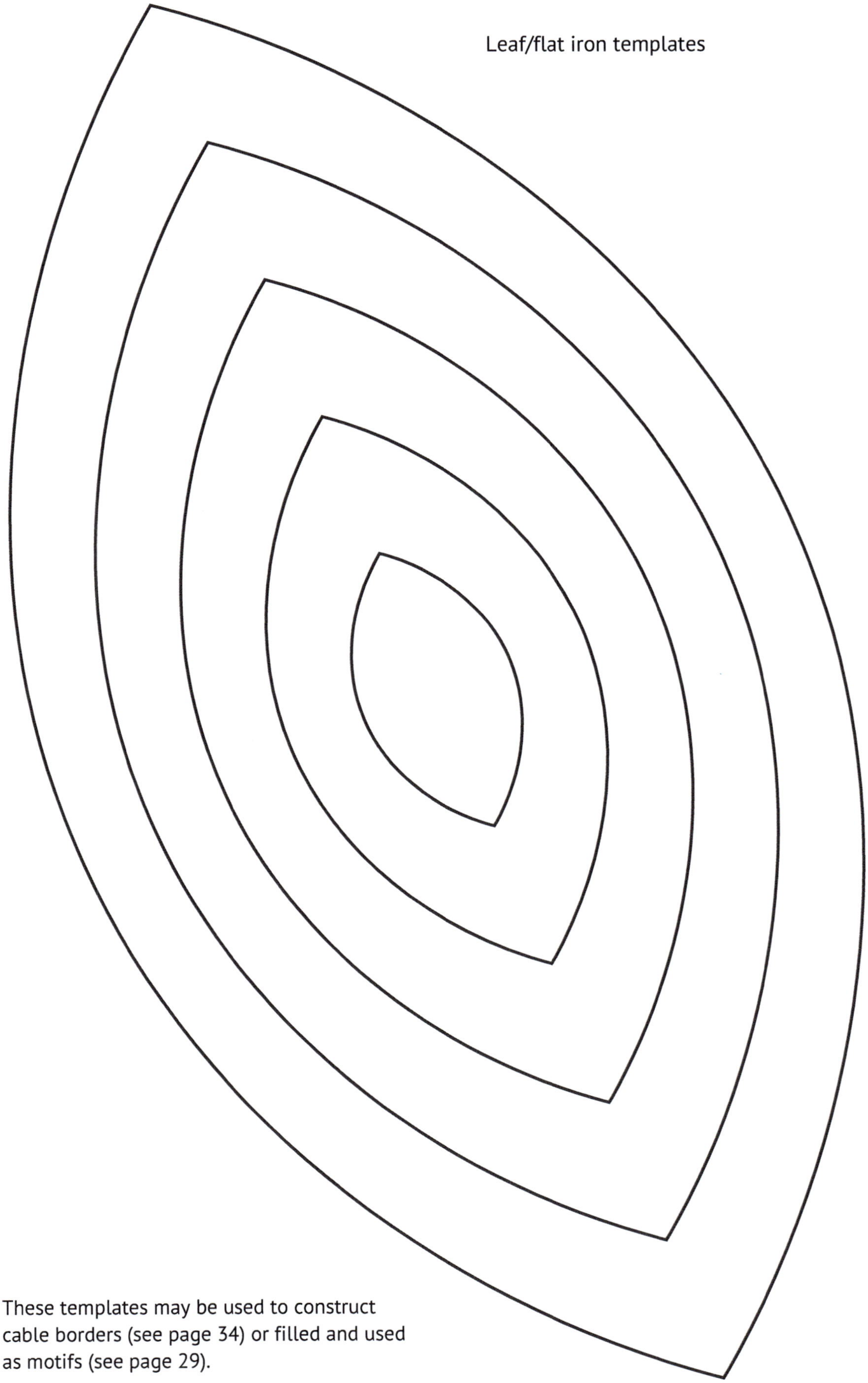

These templates may be used to construct cable borders (see page 34) or filled and used as motifs (see page 29).

Circle templates

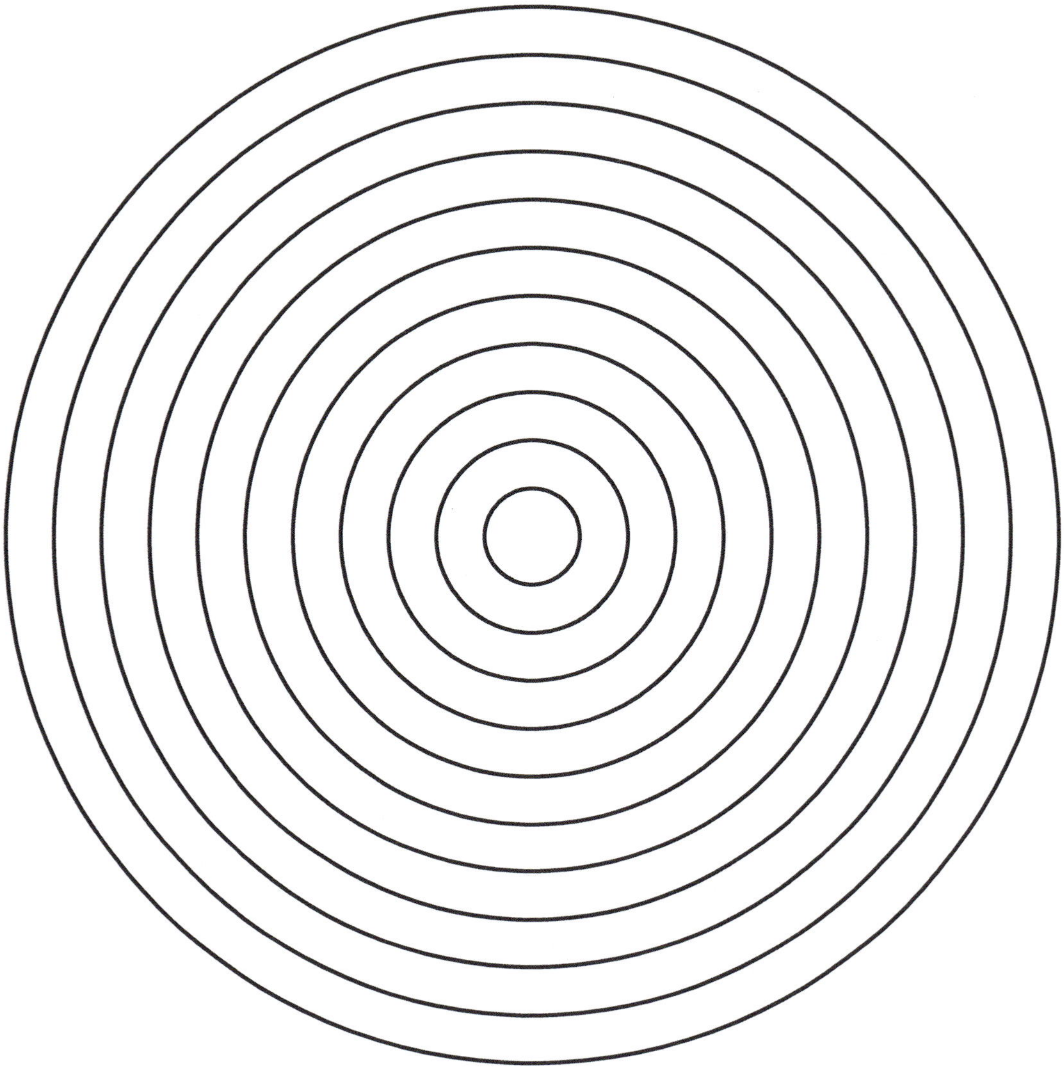

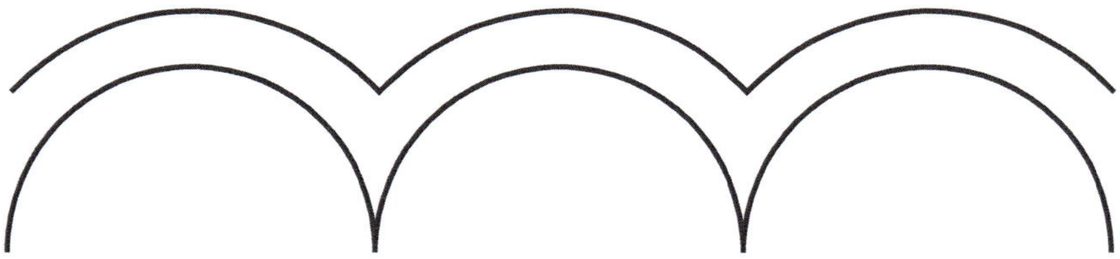

Clamshell border

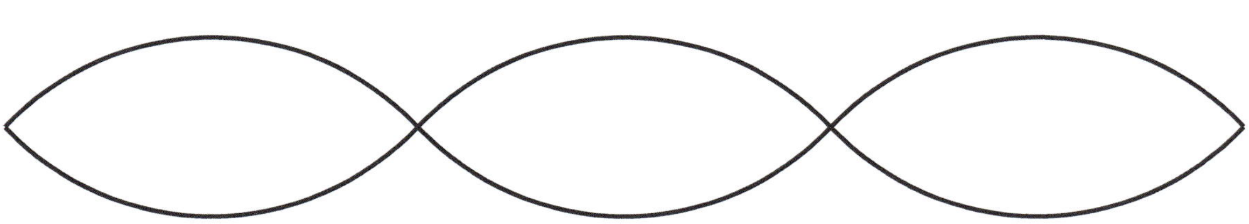

Small cable border

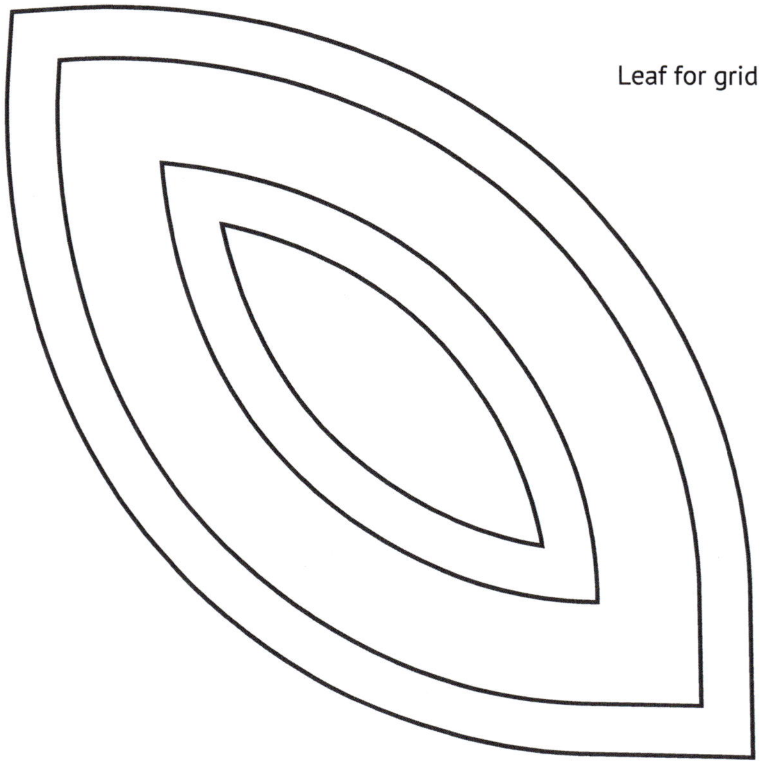

Leaf for grid designs

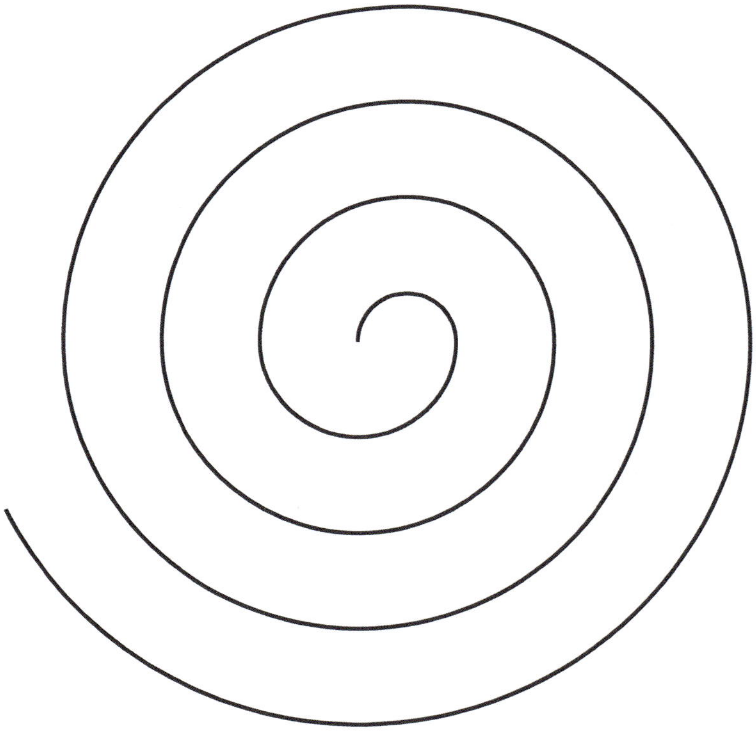

Spiral for grid designs

Heart for grid designs

Cardiganshire heart

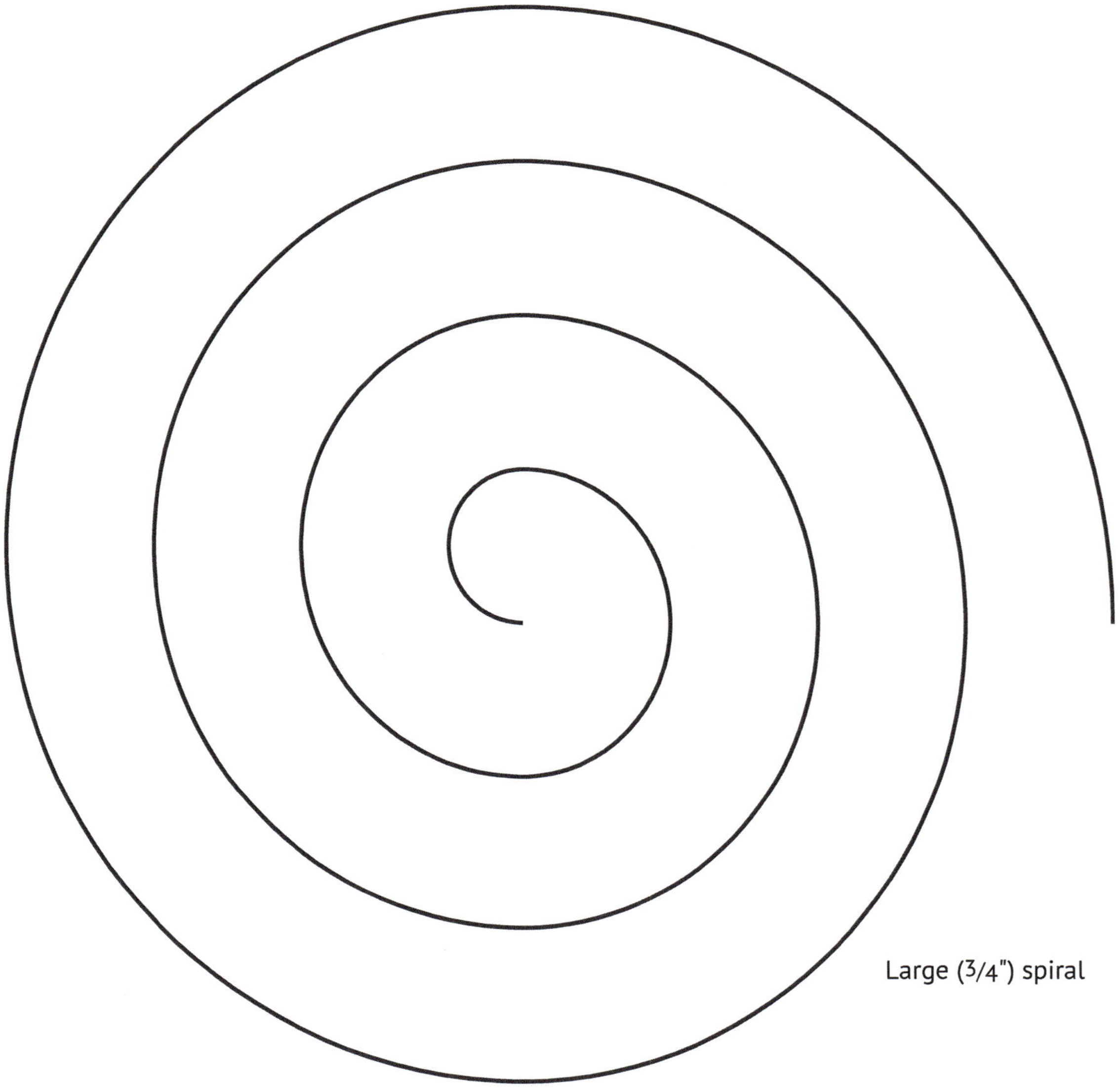

Large (3/4") spiral

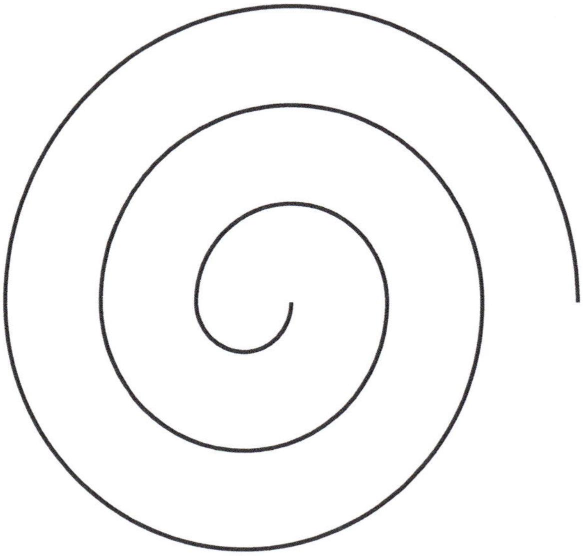

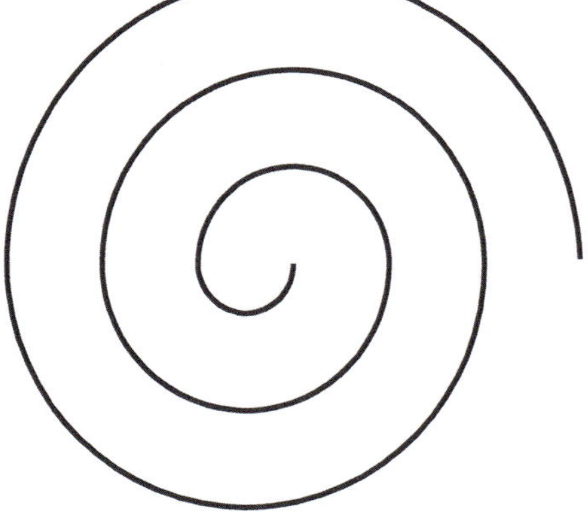

Small (3/8") spiral

Medium (1/2") spiral

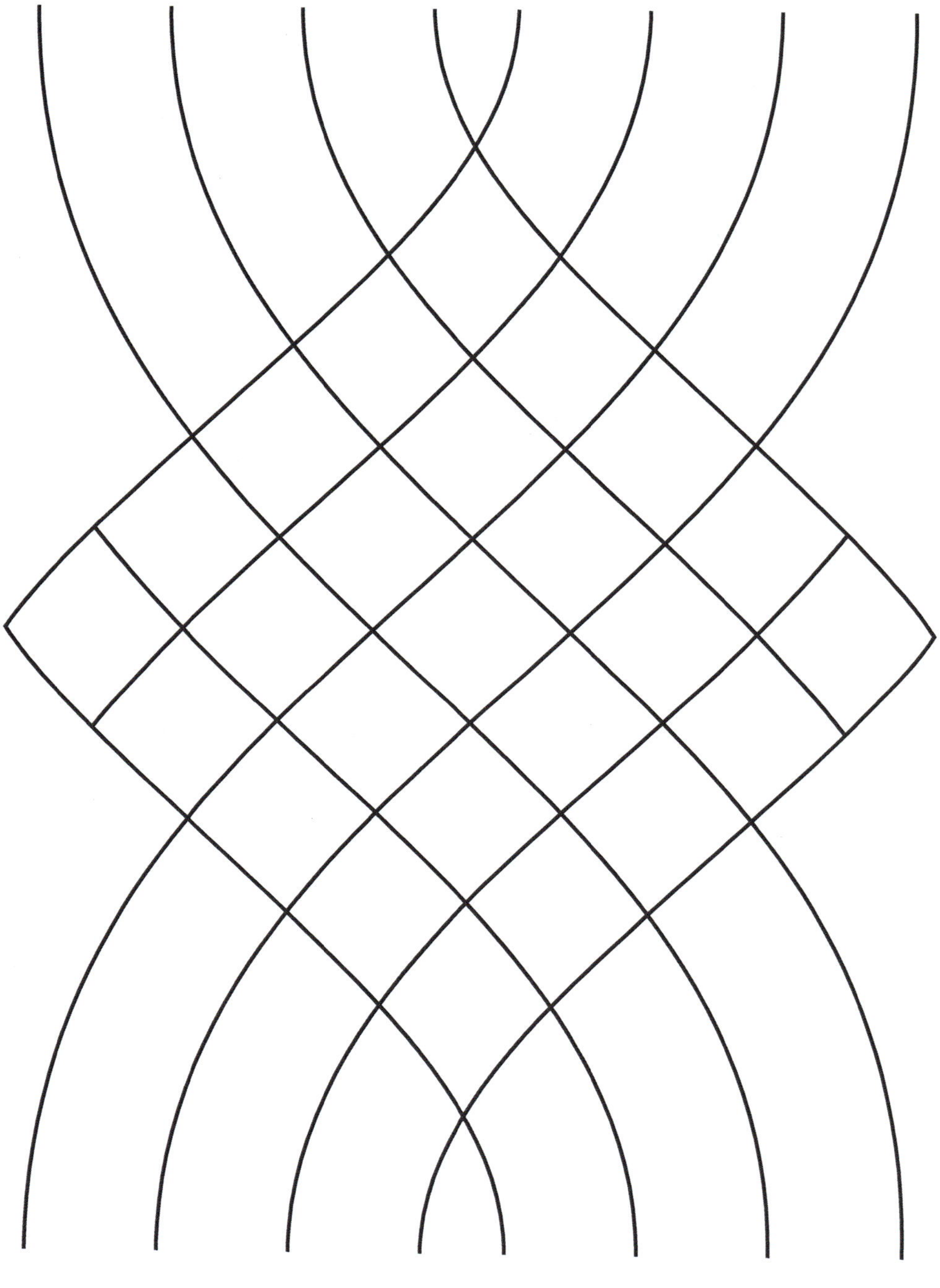

Welsh trail border

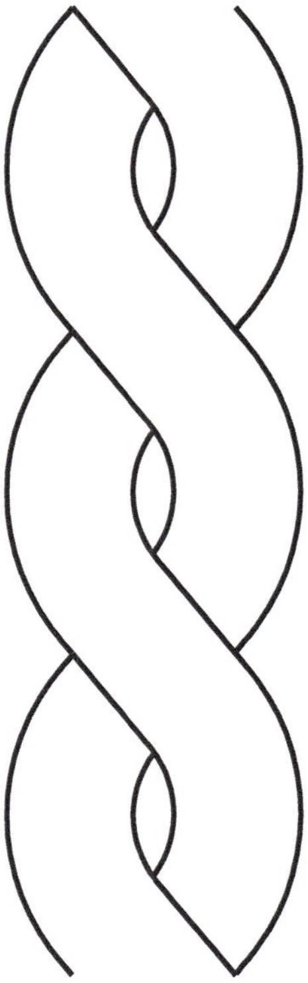

Small cable

Celtic knot

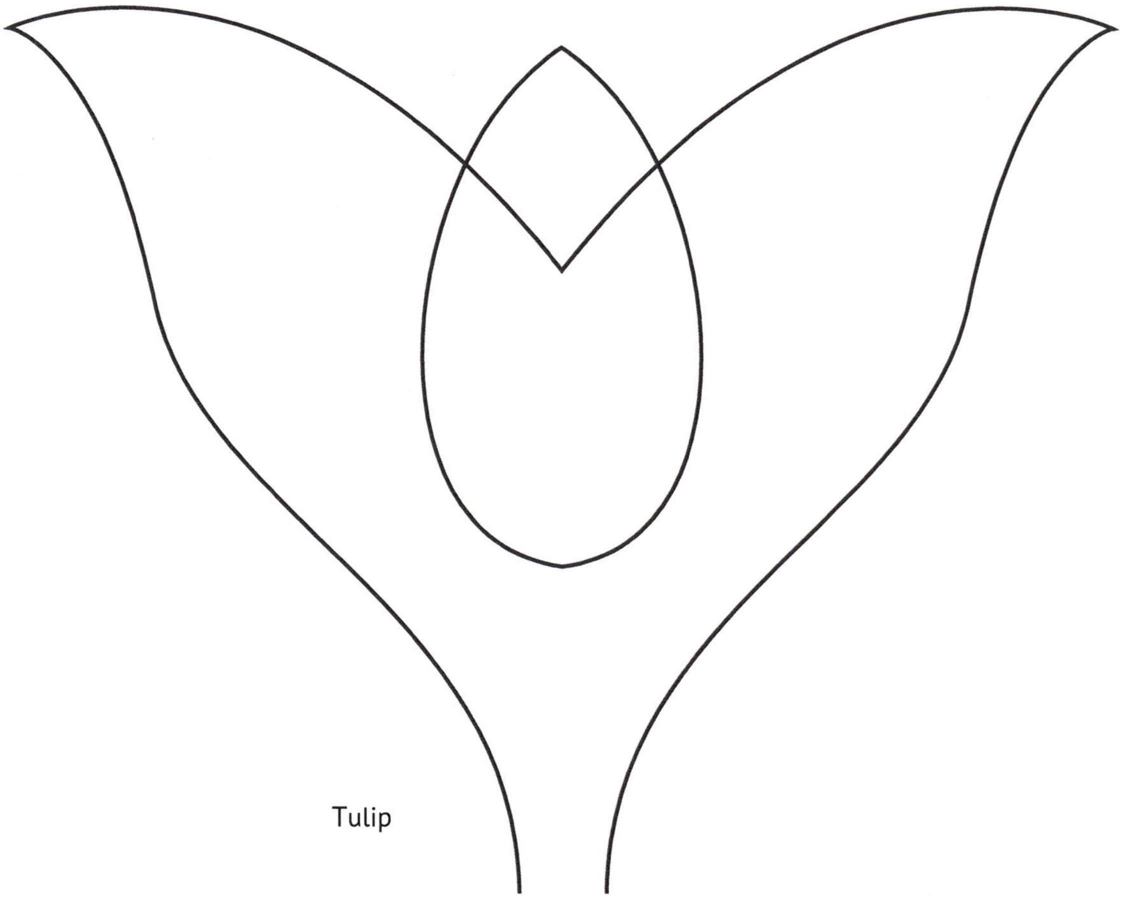

Tulip

Small rose

Narrow bent leaf

Bent leaf and spiral

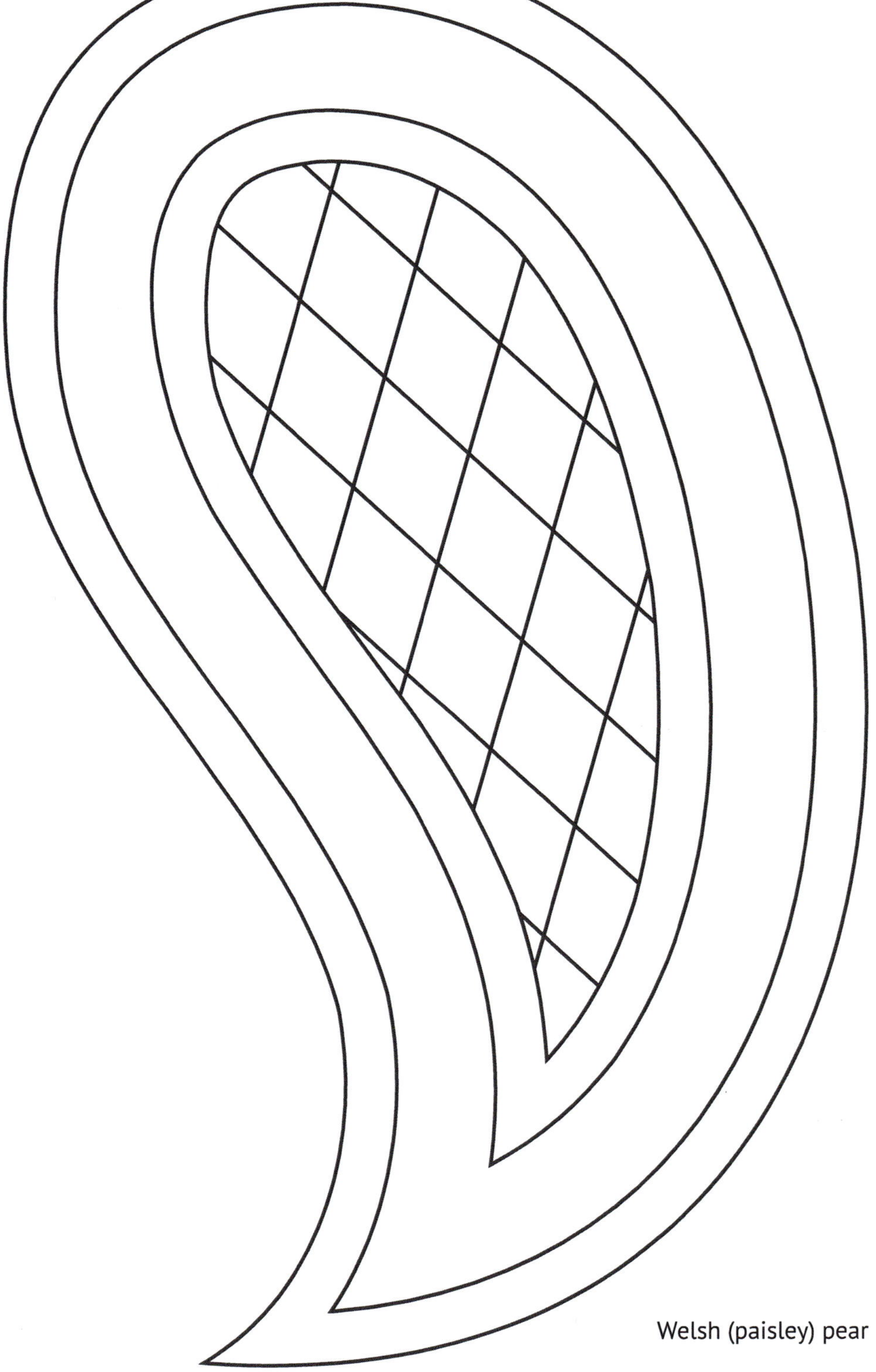

Welsh (paisley) pear

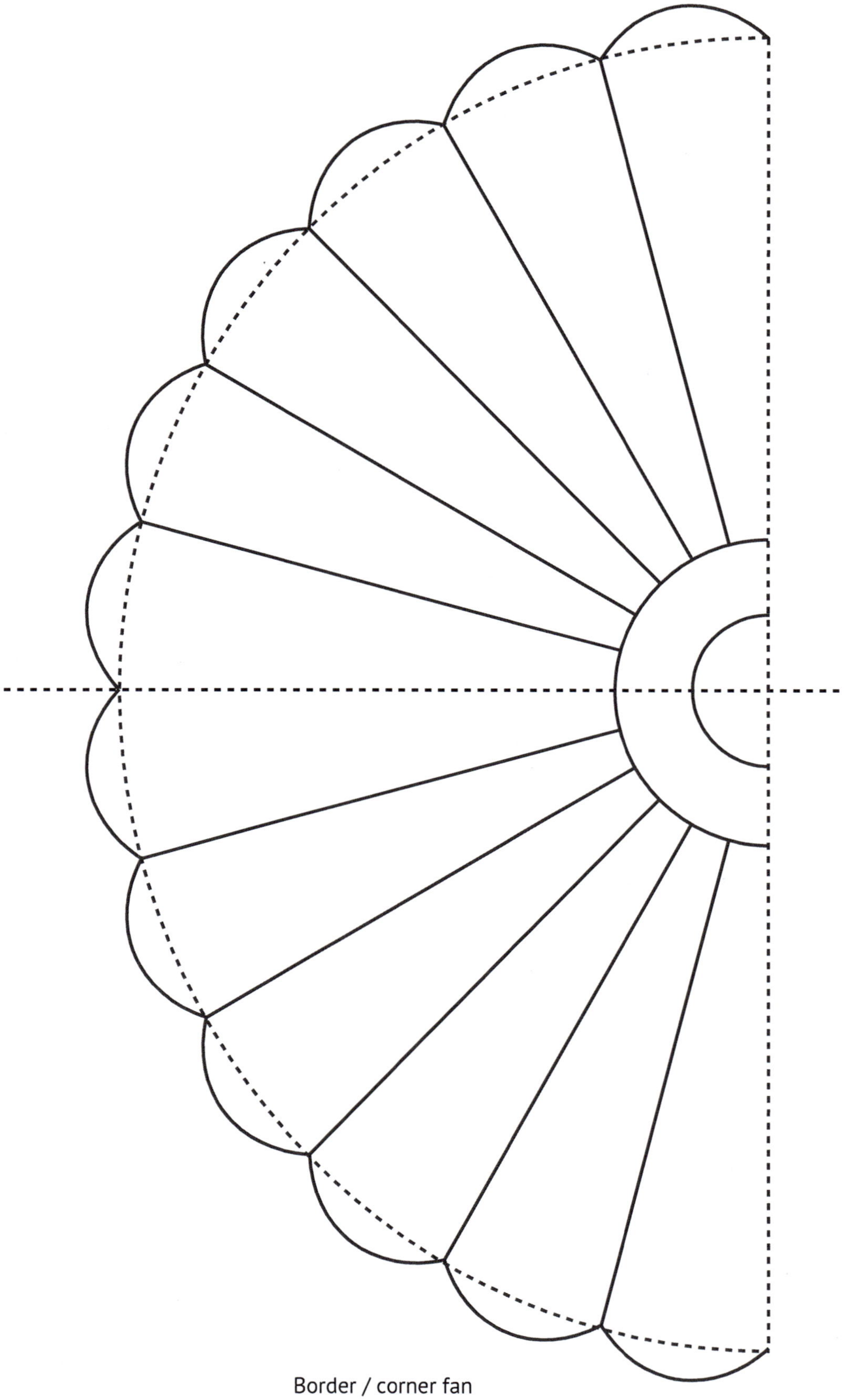

Border / corner fan

Small church window border

Further Reading

Colby, Averil (1972) ◊ Quilting ◊ Batsford, London

Chainey, Barbara (1995) ◊ The Essential Quilter ◊ David and Charles, Devon

FritzRandolph, Mavis (1954) ◊ Traditional Quilting ◊ Batsford, London

FritzRandolph, M and Fletcher, F (1955) ◊ Quilting Traditional Methods and Design ◊ Dryad Press, Leicester

Horton, Marjorie (1999) ◊ Welsh Quilting Pattern and Design Book ◊ The Welsh Quilt Centre, Lampeter

Jones, Jen (2016) ◊ Welsh Quilts. ◊ Seren, Bridgend

Jones, Jen (2005) ◊ Les Quilts Gallois (Welsh Quilts) ◊ Quiltmania, France

Lodge, Diana (1995) ◊ Quilts ◊ Mitchell Beasley, London

Osler, Dorothy (1987) ◊ Traditional British Quilts ◊ Batsford, London

Quilters' Guild of the British Isles (1995) ◊ Quilt Treasures ◊ Deidre McDonald, London

Rae, Janet (1987) ◊ Quilts of the British Isles ◊ McDonald Books, London

Stevens, Christine (1993) ◊ Quilts ◊ Gomer Press, Llandysul

Places to Visit

Jen Jones Quilts and Blankets

Pontbrendu, Llanybydder SA40 9UJ

Tel: 01750 480610

www.jen-jones.com

The Quilt Association (seasonal)

Minerva Arts Centre Llanidloes SY18 6BY

Tel: 01686 413467

www.quilt.org.uk

Melin Teifi (National Woollen Mill)

Drefach, Felindre, Llandysul SA44 5UP

Tel: 01559 371003

www.melinteifi.com

St Fagans National Museum of History

Cardiff, CF5 6XB

Tel: 0300 111 2 333

www.museum.wales/stfagans

Printed in Dunstable, United Kingdom

68272966R00094